Praise & Worship Unleashed Series Vol #2
WORSHIP: The Foundation
For Servants of the Worship Arts Ministry

Doris Stokes Knight

Praise & Worship Unleashed Series Vol. #2
WORSHIP: The Foundation
For Servants of the Worship Arts Ministry

by: Doris Stokes Knight

BPE Word Publishing
(A Division of Black Pearl Enterprises)

WORSHIP: The Foundation
For Servants of the Worship Arts Ministry
ISBN - 13: 978-1466487567
ISBN - 10: 1466487569

Printed in the United States of America
Copyright © 2013 by Doris Stokes Knight
Official Website: **www.bpewordpublishing.wix.com/Kingdombooks**
Contact Email: **bpewordpublishing@gmail.com**

Published by:
BPE Word Publishing
(A Division of Black Pearl Enterprises)

Any reference to the person of satan or the devil **IS PURPOSEFULLY NOT** capitalized in this text; as we **DO NOT** give honor or any respect to him, even in regards to grammatically addressing him correctly.

Dedications

I'd like to dedicate this book to the following people who have enriched my life so much to better understand just who I am and am supposed to be in God's Kingdom:

My Mother, **Bernice Bradfield Stokes:** who has been a constant in my life and introduced me and my siblings to the Lord as children. Thank you Mother for making attending church in our home a STANDARD and a requirement on Sunday mornings. We never had to wonder what we were doing on any given Sunday, because we already KNEW it was going to include being at the house of Worship! I love you for being the manifestation of the Proverbs 31 woman that I grew up knowing and watching all the days of my life right in our own home. God certainly knew what He was doing when He assigned you to be our Mother; **I COULD NOT** have hand-picked a better one myself. I love you to LIFE!

To my Son, **Nouri Elijah Marcellus Stokes:** for being the bright light that brought me back out of a very dark pit in my life. Being your Mother has been a sheer joy and watching you grow into the fine and fruitful young man that God is developing you into is an even greater gift. Although I raised you as a single parent and did the absolute best I could do for you, my prayers over your life were (and are) what maintained us and God has kept every promise over your life that I've prayed including watching you earn your first college degree!

The world has NO IDEA who you are going to be yet, but God's timing will manifest it. I can't think of anything I wouldn't do for you and one of those is to offer unconditional love toward you for the balance of my days.

To my childhood BFF, **Alvieno Stinson**: for being a phenomenal (platonic) friend since my childhood. We've been there and supported each other through all of our life's experiences; we have truly been through so much together. I think we have tried to demonstrate to each other what true friendship is all about. Even with all you have endured through your illness, you are an undeniable inspiration to so many including your own children. You have demonstrated your stamina, determination, intelligence and yes your "only Al" sense of humor to all who come to know you. Although I realize true friends are hard to come by, you are my oldest and dearest. I love you and "still believe" God is gonna work a miracle in you!

To my Husband **Bruce Knight**: for being the rock of our marriage and my best friend. You truly are one of the hardest working men on the planet and I appreciate the very day the Lord allowed you to come into my life FOR GOOD! Your ability to keep me strong during times when I appear to be *"spazzing"* out bring balance to me and all of the assignments the Lord is calling me to complete. I appreciate our friendship and our companionship to walk this journey of life together allowing God to gain the glory out of all He's blessed us with. Thank you for believing in me like no one else ever has. We're *"Knights for Life!"* and I love you dearly!

Table of Contents

To check the answers to the **"WORSHIP"** Quiz, just look in the back of this book on **Page 101** to see how you did!

Acknowledgments

To **my Lord and Savior Jesus Christ** whom I have committed the balance of my life to heralding Your goodness and Your awesomeness toward me and in the earth. I love You for teaching me so much about You and the lessons will continue on as long as I live. Your loving kindness toward me is unmatched; it is truly an honor to be chosen as one of your vessels to teach and spread the Gospel of Jesus Christ to all nations and to those that are serving or desire to serve in the worship arts ministry in any capacity. I absolutely owe you **EVERYTHING!** May all you've assigned for me to do to bring You glory, be acceptable in Your sight and received as the sacrifice of praise that I'm offering it as. With my whole heart...I love you.

To my Editor, **Professor LaVerne Summerlin**, you are a certified **MASTER** at your craft Ma'am and I thank you for challenging me through the medium and gift of writing to go deeper into my work, while keeping it as simple as possible so the readers the Lord has assigned to my literary works will understand its content and walk away feeling more knowledgeable and empowered about this most important ministry than before they read them.

You have been a true and total blessing to my life and I'm so glad we were able to work together to bring these materials to life and to the Kingdom of God. Your multiplied years of experience in being an Educator at the college level, inspires me to build my skill and ability to become an even better author. Your personal, hands-on mentorship in helping develop me in my approach to writing my first two books, has been an experience no college course could have taught me. I thank you with my whole heart Professor and friend; I'm already excited and looking forward to the **NEXT** volume of the series!

To my Overseeing Leadership: **Apostle Eunique Collier,** what can I say about you other than **THANK YOU** from the bottom of my heart? Thank you first of all, for believing in me and recognizing the gifts the Lord placed inside of me to share with the nations and with the Body of Christ. As you know, there were **MANY TIMES** that we had long talks about the direction that God was taking my life and the ministry I carry. You were so instrumental in helping me to see clearly how God may gift you in one area while all along fully intending to develop other areas inside of you that He sees as an opportunity for Him to gain glory in as well.

You helped me to understand that the only reason any of us are truly GREAT is because of WHOM we represent and come in the Name of. What a warrior of God you are Apostle and I thank you from the deepest part of my heart for being in my life! After God instructed you to offer blessings over me to walk in the Office of a Pastor in order to serve the Kingdom at large, it has become one of the greatest honors of my life to continue serving and being used by God as He sees fit. Thank you Mother Eunique for believing in me when I was struggling to do so myself. I love you dearly.   **~Pastor Doris Stokes Knight**

WORSHIP: The Foundation for Servants of the Worship Arts Ministry

Introduction

It is with great honor and pleasure that I take this opportunity to try and share some of the awesome revelations and teachings that the Lord has given me concerning the specific music ministry of **Praise and Worship.** It is a most misunderstood ministry at best, but with a clear understanding of its basis and Biblical beginnings, it can be one of the most liberating and rewarding areas of ministry to adopt as a **lifestyle.** As a praise and worship leader, I don't' take ministry of any kind lightly or for granted without regard to the fact that I myself must answer to our Maker about what I share with you concerning the Biblical truths behind what this area of ministry is really supposed to be about as well as how it pertains to offering God's people music ministry.

God makes it clear that He desires to "inhabit the praises of His people..." which means His heart's desire is to abide, live or take up residence with us internally. We gain God's attention by giving Him praise for who He is. He wants to be the sole reason that we DO offer Him our praises and worship; without any impure motives or hidden agendas. He truly wants our hearts and minds to be so in tune with Him, that we will avail ourselves to be vessels that can be worthily utilized by Him. He yearns for us to be yielded in our wills, so that His purpose may shine clearly through us for everyone to see Him in us!

To me, there is no greater honor or privilege than to be called to be a Worshiper.

It's a calling of distinction, uniqueness and of the highest order. Worshipers are one people that God works through in order to get His purpose accomplished in the earth realm.

If He can find a Worshiper, He can move mightily to deliver, save and set free His people from all manner of sin and evil. The Bible declares in John 4:23 that, *"But the hour cometh, and now is, when the true **worshipers** shall worship the Father in spirit and in truth: for the Father seeketh such to worship him."* In other words, He is **PURPOSEFULLY** looking for worshipers in order to carry out specific orders that others wouldn't do or would question BEFORE actually carrying out the assignment. Having the heart and spirit of a worshiper is **MANDATORY** in order to be effective in the worship arts ministry in any capacity.

This book, however, will focus on the **basic knowledge** that any person serving in any area of the worship arts ministry **SHOULD** know backwards and forwards. When we are called to serve in ANY area of ministry, we should strive to learn and know all we can about that ministry in order for us to be as effective as possible in the Kingdom and in what God is equipping us to do. We should be careful in making sure we are ONLY operating in the area of ministry we are truly Anointed for. Only God can give a person a true Anointing for any area of ministry service. The Bible says: *"**Study** to shew thyself approved unto God, a workman that needeth not to be ashamed, rightly dividing the word of truth."* 2 Timothy 2:15. (KVJ). Therefore, even the Father wants us to be WELL versed in our abilities to be servants of the Kingdom; not just some overly ambitious, zealous saints going off half-cocked knowing and trying to share half truths.

In this book, I want to walk with you step-by-step through this process of gaining a CLEAR understanding about the ministry that you are either serving in or desire to. I don't mind making it as simple as possible for you to comprehend because if I don't, what would be the point in writing the book at all? It is written from the standpoint that you may be just exploring your way through to find out IF God is truly calling you for service into one of the areas of the worship arts.

This book will cover some **BASIC PRINCIPLES** that you as a servant in the worship arts arena (if you are already in service to) **SHOULD** already know or be aware of. If you find that you don't, then GOD BLESS YOU for desiring to raise your level of understanding to know more about what you're doing. Investing in this book will help take your knowledge and wisdom to operate in your calling to an even HIGHER dimension. Knowing the history and origins of a thing helps us to better prepare for how we should be or operate in it today. History gives us a better understanding of where things came from, why things may be the way they are now and answers questions such as: what?...who?...when?...where?...why?...and how? When I teach workshops in person, other than the outlines that I teach from, (which I do share with all of you in this book in the Table of Contents), **THE BIBLE** is the only book that I teach from. Why? Because God is the author of music, the music ministry and where the whole phenomenon of music comes from....it's Him. I would think that consulting the Word of God would be the **FIRST PLACE** you should look to find how He would desire for us to be worshiping Him.

Contrary to popular belief, serving in music ministry is not just about the latest songs on Billboard's charts, or you singing your favorite Gospel artists' music, hearing your favorite song on the radio, or showing off how many riffs, runs and vocal acrobatics you can do with your voice.

That's all good, but in order to be better at WHAT you do in the worship arts ministry, you first have to make sure you have been CALLED to a specific area and that you are or have developed an intimate relationship with God the Father; that's where your power to operate in your gift will come from. Then avail yourself to what He wants from us according to His word. Will this take time? Of course, but you will find that if you make it a **LIFESTYLE**, it gets easier and better every day until it becomes a habit. **Communing** with God will become a priority for you, just like **praying** everyday should be.

What's the difference between communing and praying? Well, when we **commune** with God that insinuates intimacy and worship. It's our private moments spent in His presence where the Bible declares "there is fullness of joy!" There is a closeness you feel to the Creator that you don't experience with anyone else. With the focus solely on Him, your entire being comes into a place of desiring ONLY that which will bring Him glory and honor with your life. It's all about what does He want from you and how can you provide that?

On the other hand, **prayer** while it's powerful as well, is our gateway to speaking to God about what we go through, what we may be experiencing, going before Him on behalf of the needs of friends and loved ones, those in the Kingdom or even our own needs and yes offering our words and sentiments of thanksgiving unto Him just for who He is to us.

Prayer is our way to petition God; to implore Him to act on our behalf or to make our requests known fervently. But before you end prayer, you should ALWAYS acknowledge Jesus as Lord and as the God He is by letting Him know that He is the source and the ONLY one who is worthy of your praise, of your worship or for you to come before to be heard.

And with Him hearing you, you have faith to believe He will act. The act of thanksgiving and faith in Him to move on your behalf is what MOVES the hand of God. You will find that the Anointing on your life will increase and become more powerful when you are operating in your gift in public and maintaining your relationship with the Father through fasting, prayer, communing and reading the Word, daily in private.

The referencing content of this reading will be the King James Version of the Bible with noted diversions should I decide to utilize another translation; however, I will share some personal experiences here and there to allow you to understand my perspective on the topics being discussed.

It is an **AWESOME EXPERIENCE** to be utilized by God through His precious Anointing in service to the Kingdom when ushering in His presence among the saints! It is my sincere prayer that this book, which is actually my worship arts workshop in written format, will bless your lives and that you will be even more enlightened as to the validity, need and purpose of the ministry of praise and worship to exist within our local assemblies but more importantly, in our daily lives. Prayerfully, something in this work will help you in your walk and desire to serve God with your Temple where He longs to dwell.

So....let's get started by taking a **WORSHIP Pop Quiz** to see what you may already know (or not know). GET READY to expand your mental understanding of this FANTASTIC ministry, no matter in what capacity you may already serve or pray to serve.

~**Pastor Doris Stokes Knight**

Pre- Worship Pop Quiz!

True or False?

1.   In the Old Testament, Aaron was in charge of the construction of the Tabernacle.   ____

2.   Worshipers are **Anointed** by their pastors.   ____

3.   An **effective worship leader** always makes sure each of the praise team members' outfits are color-coordinated.   ____

4.   **Moses** was the designer of the Old Testament Tabernacle.   ____

5.   The **"Holy of Holies"** is where the High Priest lived.   ____

6.   I qualify to be a **worship leader** as long as I can either read music or play an instrument.   ____

7.   God reserved praise & worship for the music department of our local churches.   ____

8.   The Ark of the Covenant was welcomed by all who saw it.   ____

9.   Obed-edom was afraid of the Ark of the Covenant, therefore it was taken to King David's house to reside for three months.   ____

10.   Consecration is not a requirement that needs to be met in order to worship God.   ____

11.   The Ark of the Covenant is where Noah lived.   ____

12.   The desire for true worship begins inside of our own selves.   ____

*To check the answers to the **"WORSHIP"** Quiz, just look in the back of this book on **Page 101** to see how you did!

You may also check the Author's Website for the answers at:
www.bpewordpublishing.wix.com/Kingdombooks

CHAPTER 1

WHAT PRAISE AND WORSHIP <u>ARE NOT!</u>
Dispelling Myths and Untruths about the Ministry of Praise & Worship

"...Let everything that has breath, praise the Lord. Praise ye the Lord."

Psalm 150 (KJV)

Over the years, when I ask people the simple question of what they think the praise and worship ministry IS or what is it truly about, their responses are....well....staggering! Here are some of them from previous students who have taken my workshops:

- "Praise and worship at our church is when we let the very best singers show what they got!"
- "I think it's when the Deacons pray and get on one knee to hit the seats."
- "Praise and worship is usually when we get to sing the best songs during church service!"
- "Praise and worship is when we sing two fast songs and maybe one slow song before the morning worship service begins."
- "Praise and worship is the time when you get the congregation riled up and people are running around the church praisin' God!"
- "Praise and worship is when the team comes out in those really nice outfits that match. They look so nice; I pray one day I'll be able to sing with them."

One of the things the Lord dealt with me about upon taking on the assignment of being one of the Educators in Biblical teaching for this particular area of ministry, is that He didn't want me to conduct workshops where I go teach some songs to a choir or group of people and in a couple days they end up giving a "feel good" concert. Not that it's so much anything wrong with that, but He was making something VERY CLEAR to me; He wasn't calling ME to do that. The Spirit of the Lord said: *"Daughter, there are enough people doing music workshops; what I REALLY want is someone who will be a Champion for me, in helping to educate my servants that carry the Anointed assignment to serve in the worship arts to find out through my Word what it is that I WANT from them as worshipers!"*

WOW! You can imagine what a revelation that was to me; I felt like, I guess that WOULD be the best way to know how to please Him, is by Biblically researching and learning through His Word how He desires to be praised, desires to be worshiped and desires to dwell among His people.....again, **Biblically!** This meant that He was requiring more of me to study and research through the Word what this whole thing is truly about. This is what I've found to be **MYTHS** about the ministry of praise & worship:

*It is **NOT** a tempo of song; praise = uptempo, worship = medium to slow.

In actuality, the tempo of the song has nothing to do with whether it's praise or worship. A song of praise can be either, as well as a worship song. What determines the difference is what the song's lyrical content is speaking about and to whom. Is it a song of edification for the Saints? Is it solely about glorifying Jesus as King? Is it a song about the characteristics of Jesus? Is it a song about how GREAT Jesus is?

*It is **NOT** the same thing; they are not synonymous terms.

<u>Praise</u> IS a vehicle of faith which brings us into the presence & power of God. It is also spiritual weaponry. A tool used to fight the enemy! **Reference: (Psalm 150)**

<u>Worship</u> IS accessing His glory through your relationship with Him. **Reference: (John 4:24)**

*It is **NOT** something you do because all the other churches are doing it.

However, other churches may learn from your church about the praise and worship ministry and why it would be a great addition for them to add its function into their ministry for the edification of their congregation. It's nothing wrong with admiring what another ministry may be doing, but it's MORE important to understand WHY they are doing it. The Bible declares in **Proverbs 4:7**; "Wisdom is the principal thing; therefore get wisdom: and with all thy getting get understanding." Don't become a copycat just for the sake of "copycatting."

*It is **NOT** a service on Sunday morning to showcase a mere few who have decided they are the best singers in the church.

You don't necessarily have to be the best singer in the church to qualify, but harmonious singing is what makes the experience of that ministry so beautiful and engaging for the saints as well as an offering of excellence unto the Lord. On the other hand, it always helps if those that are going to be going forth can at least hold a tune, understand and know what vocal voice they sing in, are "teachable" in attitude and Spirit and be able to blend and do harmonies with the other singers.

In the Old Testament, they always speak of SKILLED singers and SKILLED musicians; why? Because the Lord wanted those with the God-given ability (what He's given to them), to give it back to Him as a sacrifice of their praise. Our gifts were not given for ourselves; our gifts are given to us to give to others. Have you ever received a gift on Christmas, and the person that gave it to you asked for it back? **Reference: 1 Chronicles 15:22** More than likely, not.

*It is **NOT** shouting all over the church in the "Holy Ghost"

Now when praise and worship are going forth with POWER, that's not to say that may not happen! It certainly can, but that's not the DEFINITION of praise and/or worship. That is a by-product of experiencing being in the midst of a powerful release. Shouting is not prohibited, however it's encouraged; but it's a part of the manifestations of His presence in the midst of the praise being presented as well as: dancing **(Psalm 30:11);** clapping **(Psalm 47:1),** and rejoicing **(Psalm 118:15).**

*It is **NOT** about YOU at all!

It think this is important to note, because what I see going on frequently are things like the students responses I listed above and it turns the attention away from what that ministry is actually *"supposed"* to be about. If anything other than Jesus Christ is the center or focus of a praise and worship period, then those are only distractions that **SHOULD NOT** be. No flesh shall ever glory in the presence of God; it simply CAN'T be about us. **Reference: (1 Corinthians 1:29).**

Only when it is being presented as a means of edification to the Body, but that speaks ABOUT us, not puts the focus on us. If outfits, whether shoes are matching or not, women or men not dressed appropriately, are more important or are receiving more attention than the actual focus of whether God is getting the praise He so worthily deserves, in all sincerity, it should not be allowed and should be considered **out of order.**

HEART CHECK!

None of the above is intended to offend you but IT IS intended to help give you a desire to change your mindset (and heart) about how you may have previously thought about the worship arts ministry. Throughout this book, I will be doing **HEART CHECKS** from time to time, so that if you read something that you either have never heard of before OR that may hit you in your heart in an offensive manner, that you'll willfully turn over that spirit to the Lord so He can cleanse you from wrong thinking, wrong motives, wrong actions (previously) and that you will allow Him to transform your mind and heart toward How HE wants to use you as a vessel of praise or worship for His glory.

Getting rid of pride, which dwells in the heart (or soul realm) takes maturity and willingness to release it on your own. He's just using me, through the vehicle of this book to hopefully get you there so you may develop into the BEST vessel of honor that the Father FULLY intended for you to be! The TRUTH does hurt sometimes, but you know what they say: *"It may be tight....but it's RIGHT!"*

Now that we've discussed the myth aspects of what praise and worship **ARE NOT**, let's talk more in depth about what it actually IS. I pray the following chapters will be an enlightening blessing for you.

CHAPTER 1

NOTES

CHAPTER 2

WORSHIP 101 – WHAT IS WORSHIP?

"Give unto the Lord the glory due His name; bring an offering and come before Him; worship the Lord in the beauty of holiness."

~*1 Chronicles 16:29*

As it relates to God, Worship is the **privilege** of those who seek God with clean hands and a pure heart. **Clean hands** refers to our lifestyle of living holy; our intentional purpose of living in such a way on a daily basis that it becomes a part of our character. Have no purposeful dealings in wrongdoings, lasciviousness, unrighteousness and the like. The Bible reminds us in I Thessalonians 5:2 to "Abstain from all appearance of evil." In other words, the more you allow your name or your reputation to be associated with negative events, negative people, people of low or no moral character, the more their reputation will be attributed to you. Keep your hands, minds, mouth and the like as far away from that type of behavior and those characteristics as possible.

A Pure heart on the other hand is speaking about our thought and heart processes toward others, toward God and even towards ourselves. If it's possible, always try to see the good in people. Sometimes people may not always do the right things, but their hearts were in the right place. Make a purposeful point to stay away from gossipers, backbiters, troublemakers, whose negative character can influence your heart toward others or certain situations. Allow God to always be your navigation as it pertains to those you encounter or have to deal with on a regular basis. Be open but always protect your heart. We must be like David in Psalm 51:10 constantly asking God to create in us a clean heart and to renew our spirits with righteousness.

As it pertains to God, and as you develop your personal relationship with Him, you will find that He will begin to expand your faith in Him. What do you mean? Well, early in my relationship with God, I would believe God for simple things and He would come through and do it. But looking back, I see that was His way of getting me to build my faith IN HIM and to know that He would come through for me. However, as I got older, I noticed that He would not always answer when I thought He should, but nonetheless He would work out whatever my circumstances were for my good. Now that I'm at this point in my life, there are seasons He will be silent for long periods of time, or speak in very different ways or through people I would've never expected, but STILL making it clear to me that He's with me, He's for me and He hears my prayers. Having a pure heart toward God will require you to always know that He has your best interest in mind. It's imperative as you continue to get to know Him as Lord, that you recognize His traits, His personality, His character and His methods of operation. Even if He doesn't answer you when YOU think He should, or how YOU think He should, just know however He works it out, it will benefit you in the end. Always KNOW in your heart that He's for you!

There are requirements to being able to worship God. He is very demanding in how we access Him; or come into His presence. **You MUST qualify to be in God's presence.**

Psalm 100:2 "Serve the LORD with gladness: come before his presence with singing." (a Tehillah praise (singing) permits no thought other than God!)
The **POSTURE** of worship: to bow oneself down in adoration and contemplation of God.

HOW DO I QUALIFY TO GET INTO HIS PRESENCE?

According to God's Word, He does have requirements in order to gain access into His presence. And **since He's sovereign**, He reserves that right to do so. Instead of taking a stance of offense, see if you can notice yourself in some of the following points AND how you may make a conscious effort or decision to commit yourself to become better as a worshiper according to His desires:

*You must be holy as God is holy.

*"Speak unto all the congregation of the children of Israel, and say unto them, Ye shall be **holy**: for I the LORD your **God** am **holy**."* __Leviticus 19:2__

*"And Joshua said unto the people, Ye cannot serve the LORD: for he **is** an **holy God**; he **is** a jealous **God**; he will not forgive your transgressions nor your sins."* __Joshua 24:19__

*"Exalt ye the LORD our **God**, and worship at his footstool; for he **is holy**."* __Psalm 99:5__

*"Exalt the LORD our **God**, and worship at his **holy** hill; for the LORD our **God is holy**."* __Psalm 99:9__

In each of the above scriptures, God is making Himself the standard for us to follow. Being HOLY IS NOT a suggestion; it's a requirement. Not that we'll ever be Him, but in our daily lives, we CAN reflect Him and His spirit in us for others to see. We can take on the character of Christ where His character can literally become who we are. Since the Bible clearly declares we are made in His image, then surely we can become likened unto our Creator. If He is Holy and has chosen that as His standard for being God, then we too can be holy in our lifestyle.

God is holy for a reason. Holiness protects us from ourselves if we choose to live it out daily. It keeps us from sin and protects us from the consequences of stepping outside of the realm of the arc of safety that holiness provides to us. Living holy is our earthly ADT security system that guards our lives from transgressing against God. The benefits of living holy far outweighs the sacrifice of sin you give up for a few moments of pleasure and folly. Holiness qualifies us to be in service to Him so that others may see His glory in, on and through our lives. We never know who our lifestyle is compelling to change; it's important to be a living example and epistle of God's grace in how we live.

*You must be pure in motive.

*"He that hath clean hands, and a **pure heart**; who hath not lifted up his soul unto vanity, nor sworn deceitfully." **Psalm 24:4***

*"Let us draw near with a true **heart** in full assurance of faith, having our **heart**s sprinkled from an evil conscience, and our bodies washed with **pure** water."* **Hebrews 10:22**

*"Seeing ye have purified your souls in obeying the truth through the Spirit unto unfeigned love of the brethren, see that ye love one another with a **pure heart** fervently:"* **1 Peter 1:22**

*"Now the end of the commandment is charity out of a **pure heart**, and of a good conscience, and of faith unfeigned:"* **1 Timothy 1:5**

Believe it or not, God knows when we are doing things from our heart and when we are doing things ONLY to benefit from it ourselves. That's not to say there's anything wrong with us benefitting from making great decisions.

But if your only reason for EVER doing anything kind or out of the way for someone else is so that you can be the one to reap the benefit, that IS NOT an act of kindness from the heart; it's not genuine. The motive is selfish in its very essence.

If you truly desire to bless someone else, it shouldn't be based on whether you get something back or not, but that God may be glorified in your giving to that person, situation or circumstance. One of my favorite Psalms is 51:10; we must always ask the Lord to create in us a PURE and clean heart and renew in us a spirit of righteousness. This also helps to govern our behavior as well as our souls.

*You must have clean hands and a pure heart and truth in your innermost being.

*"He that loveth **pureness** of **heart**, for the grace of his lips the king shall be his friend." **Proverbs 22:11**

*"Blessed are the **pure** in **heart**: for they shall see God." **Matthew 5:8**

Please review my comments at the very beginning of this chapter.

*You must live a consecrated life.

*"And the LORD said unto Moses, Go unto the people, and sanctify them to day and to morrow, and let them wash their clothes," **Exodus 19:10**

*"And let the priests also, which come near to the LORD, sanctify themselves, lest the LORD break forth upon them." **Exodus 19:22**

"Sanctify yourselves therefore, and be ye holy: for I am the LORD your God. And ye shall keep my statutes, and do them: I am the LORD which sanctify you."
Leviticus 20:7-8

Living a holy and consecrated life simply means one that is dedicated to serving the Lord in your full being. In your speech, your actions and behaviors, the use of your gifts and time, the way you treat your spouse, children, church, friends, on and on. Living a life that is set apart from the norm or from the way average people choose to live is a choice. Although you may know others who may be involved in all manner of evil or questionable lifestyles, those types of choices cannot be options for you as a true worshiper of God. God is the standard setter, so the requirements are set and come directly from Him.

It becomes evident to others if someone is or isn't walking or living in holiness. The choice to live holy affects your outward appearance as well as your inward being. Even if others don't know the details, they can tell when you are or are not living a life of character and holiness and peace.

*You must have your heart cleansed from all evil that has taken up residence there, living a life of truth and purity.

[1]Lord, who shall abide in thy tabernacle? who shall dwell in thy holy hill?

[2]He that walketh uprightly, and worketh righteousness, and speaketh the truth in his heart.

[3]He that backbiteth not with his tongue, nor doeth evil to his neighbour, nor taketh up a reproach against his neighbour.

[4]In whose eyes a vile person is contemned; but he honoureth them that fear the LORD. He that sweareth to his own hurt, and changeth not.

[5]He that putteth not out his money to usury, nor taketh reward against the innocent. He that doeth these things shall never be moved. **_Psalm 15_**

Truth and purity are characteristics that anyone professing a life of Christ *should* have, however, those that claim worshiper status most definitely should exude these qualities. When you understand that you don't own yourself and that you represent the Creater of the universe, you begin to view things from a totally different perspective. It's like in the lyrics to the song so eloquently penned by William McDowell, "I Give Myself Away";

"My life is not my own, to you I belong, I give myself,

I give myself to You."

Walking our daily lives out to others is a form of worship and testament to the world as to whom it is you belong and represent.

¹The earth is the LORD's, and the fulness thereof; the world, and they that dwell therein.

²For he hath founded it upon the seas, and established it upon the floods.

³Who shall ascend into the hill of the LORD? or who shall stand in his holy place?

⁴He that hath clean hands, and a pure heart; who hath not lifted up his soul unto vanity, nor sworn deceitfully.

⁵He shall receive the blessing from the LORD, and righteousness from the God of his salvation.

⁶This is the generation of them that seek him, that seek thy face, O Jacob. Selah.
Psalm 24

I encourage you to read the **FULL** chapter of Psalm 24 and challenge yourself to commit it to memory.

³I will set no wicked thing before mine eyes: I hate the work of them that turn aside; it shall not cleave to me.

⁴A froward heart shall depart from me: I will not know a wicked person.

⁵Whoso privily slandereth his neighbour, him will I cut off: him that hath an high look and a proud heart will not I suffer.

6Mine eyes shall be upon the faithful of the land, that they may dwell with me: he that walketh in a perfect way, he shall serve me.

7He that worketh deceit shall not dwell within my house: he that telleth lies shall not tarry in my sight.

8I will early destroy all the wicked of the land; that I may cut off all wicked doers from the city of the LORD. **_Psalm 101_**

The writer in Psalm 101 (which is believed to have been written by King David) is talking about the condition of the heart. He understands that God does judge the evil that dwells within us. That's why it is BEST to try to get rid of destructive issues of the heart; petty jealousies, envy, covetousness as quickly as possible. Things that will hold you back, hinder your progress, cut off your blessings aren't worth being stagnated in your walk with God. When these types of issues are not dealt with properly or left unchecked, they lead to setting up roots of bitterness, self hatred and sometimes hatred toward anybody else that is progressing in their lives or doing better than you may be doing. Even in cases where you feel your feelings toward another are warranted and you may have been mistreated, God still makes it plain to us in Romans 12:19 that He takes full ownership of vengeance; He will make sure that those who mistreat us or come against us without reason will be dealt with. Trust God to handle them, then use your weapon of forgiveness to let them go free from your wrath. Hatred or unforgiveness lodged in your heart, especially over an extended period of time, only hurts you. The other person has gone on with their life and probably could care less that you still hold bitterness toward them.

It is imperative as a worshiper that we understand by holding on to such destructive attitudes, it will deter you from going forth in your gift effectively.

You can't be hateful AND worship God at the same time.

Ridding yourself of these feelings **BEFORE** you go before God's people in worship is crucial in not relaying or transferring that venomous spirit to those you will be ministering to.

There are many who don't realize that the role of leading worship is an extremely influential and vulnerable time during worship service. Most people come with an open heart and open spirit to receive something positive to help them get through their next week. They look forward to coming into the presence of God after dealing with all of their own personal conflicts and challenges during their work week. If the worship LEADER or praise team members aren't right in their heart, in their attitude, in their behavior, in their spirit, it can cause dangerous results to those being ministered to. They can spiritually take on what you're releasing without even being aware of it. In fact, if you find you can't relinquish your negative feelings and attitudes quickly, then at least have the respect toward God and the ministry, to sit yourself down for a season (a day, a week, a month whatever is necessary), in order to deal with your feelings of negativity. It may mean having a meeting with your Pastor, a trusted Elder, mentor or friend in your life that will be honest with you. Whatever the case, make sure you deal with it **EFFECTIVELY** before releasing any more *"ministry"* to anyone because **hurt people....hurt people.**

Maintaining bad attitudes can also lead or be the cause of other medical health issues that you'll experience in your body which is the Temple of Christ. The freedom you need to move on will come when you release others from their offense toward you. Above is a part of Psalm 101, but I highly recommend that you read the whole chapter.

HEART CHECK!

<u>WHAT DOES WORSHIP INVOLVE?</u>

Worship is an intimate relationship between a person and the creation of all mankind...God the Father. There is no such thing as worship taking place without a relationship with Him being established first.

How would you even know what He wants if you don't make it a priority of some kind to find out what He desires from you as a worshiper? It would be the same thing if someone desired to be my "friend" but we **NEVER** spent time together, I don't know anything personal about them, never met their family members, never been to their home or have any recollection of any memories I've created with them good or bad. Relationships are formed on purpose and require maintenance throughout the years, whether it's family, friends, acquaintances or work related.

While the Bible makes it clear (at least to me) that anything God has created has the ability to **PRAISE** Him in some form: *"...Let everything that has breath praise the Lord. Praise ye the Lord."* ~Psalm 150:6 **WORSHIP,** on the other hand, is based on relationship and an intentional desire to learn **HOW** to connect in a manner that is pleasing unto the Father. It is important for me to include the scripture references for my work, because again, I try to keep my opinions out of the teaching as much as possible except when sharing personal experiences with some of the content discussed, but instead direct you more toward the Word of God that will confirm and substantiate my findings, positions and thoughts. According to the Bible, REAL worship will involve:

*Devotion:

Webster's II New Riverside Dictionary decribes this word as: *Ardent attachment or loyalty; Religious zeal; piety. An act of religious observance, especially private prayer.* The Bible says it this way in several scripture texts that let's us know DEVOTION is expected from us to God the Father.

*"Then saith Jesus unto him, Get thee hence, Satan: for it is written, Thou shalt worship the Lord thy **God**, and him **only** shalt thou **serve**. __Matthew 4:10__*

*"And Jesus answered and said unto him, Get thee behind me, Satan: for it is written, Thou shalt worship the Lord thy **God**, and him **only** shalt thou **serve**."* __Luke 4:8__

Jesus knew even when being tempted by satan that God was the **ONLY GOD** to be worshiped without exception. His devotion to the Father rang clear in the scriptures listed above.

The devil was so stupid, *he thought* he was deceiving Jesus by boasting about all that he would give him if he would only bow down to him, when in actuality, **he DIDN'T OWN ANY OF THE THINGS he WAS PROMISING JESUS IN THE FIRST PLACE!**

Devotion also involves making a choice as to where your loyalties lay or are. These two scriptures remind us of that fact.

*"No man can **serve** two masters: for either he will hate the one, and love the other; or else he will hold to the one, and despise the other. Ye **cannot serve** God and **mammon**."* __Matthew 6:24__

*"No servant can **serve** two masters: for either he will hate the one, and love the other; or else he will hold to the one, and despise the other. Ye **cannot serve** God and **mammon**."* __Luke 16:13__

The scripture texts make it clear in the above verses that **NO ONE** can serve two gods. We MUST make a choice in the matter concerning our own lives; this is why they called being "saved" a personal relationship you establish with Jesus Christ. It's only based on the relationship you have and are developing with Him alone. It is proven by the manner in which you choose to live and walk out your life. Not the relationship your Mother or Grandmother had with the Lord but...**YOURS!**

*Reverence: (fear)

Webster's II Riverside Dictionary states that Reverence is: *A profound feeling of awe and respect. An expression of respect as a bow. Used as a form of address for certain members of the clergy.*

But when it comes to God the Father:

*"Wherefore we receiving a kingdom which cannot be moved, let us have grace, whereby we may serve God acceptably with **reverence** and godly fear:"* **Hebrews 12:28**

Having reverence for God is a **MUST** as a worshiper. The ultimate respect lies in knowing, appreciating and celebrating who He is.

We don't have any choices in overstepping our bounds when it comes to reverencing God. I'll talk more about how the *lack of respect* toward God got a lot of people killed in the Old Testament in the next chapter, so read on.

*Adoration:

Webster's II Riverside Dictionary says of Adoration: ***To worship as divine. To love or revere deeply.***

This definition fits in nicely with these scripture references:

*"Therefore David blessed the Lord before all the assembly and said, Be praised, **adored**, and thanked, O Lord, the God of Israel our [forefather], forever and ever."* **1 Chronicles 29:10 (AMP Version)**

*"And David said to all the assembly, Now **adore** (praise and thank) the Lord your God! And all the assembly blessed the Lord, the God of their fathers, and bowed down and did obeisance to the Lord and to the king [as His earthly representative]."* **1 Chronicles 29:20 (AMP Version)**

*"And upon hearing it, they **adored** and exalted and praised and thanked God….."* **Acts 21:20**

When you adore someone or something, it's precious to you. You care for it, look out for it and won't allow anyone to come against it. It's valuable to you and you've placed it in a position of importance in your life. God deserves our ultimate adoration as a worshiper. He must be our central focus as it pertains to the centerpiece of our worship. When we adore someone or something, we always make time for it; therefore our relationship with God can't be casual. It has to be maintained on a daily basis. The adoration we hold for Him must be constant without question.

32

*Respect:

Our dictionary (Webster's II Riverside) gives this as a definition for Respect: *To feel or show deferential regard for: to esteem. To avoid violation of or interference with. The willingness to show consideration or appreciation.*

"And Abel, he also brought of the firstlings of his flock and of the fat thereof. And the LORD had **respect** *unto Abel and to his offering:"* **Genesis 4:4**

"But unto Cain **and to his offering he had not respect. And Cain was very wroth, and his countenance fell."** Genesis 4:5

"And the LORD was gracious unto them, and had compassion on them, and had **respect** *unto them, because of his covenant with Abraham, Isaac, and Jacob, and would not destroy them, neither cast he them from his presence as yet."* **2 Kings 13:33**

"I will meditate in thy precepts, and have **respect** *unto thy ways."*

Psalm 119:15

"Though the LORD be high, yet hath he **respect** *unto the lowly: but the proud he knoweth afar off."* *Psalm 138:6*

For most of us, our first experience with learning to have and hold respect for someone came toward our parents or whomever was the caregiver over our lives when we were children. If you did something out of order, more than likely they were going to **CORRECT** you for it and it was usually in a way where you would remember never to do that particular wrong-doing again! Sometimes that came in the form of spankings, punishments, curfews, taking away things you loved or enjoyed doing and the like. Respect is earned and although when we're young and immature, we tend to think our parents are the worst people on earth, we eventually understand as we mature and get older, that they were actually THE BEST people in our lives who always had our backs and taught us right from wrong so we could understand how the "real world" works as we get older.

God is somewhat the same way.

While He may allow us to have some of the things we desire, He doesn't give us everything we want **all the time**. For instance, He knows what would happen should He allow us to have a ton of money while being immature mentally to handle the responsibility of it, a job we weren't ready for, children we don't' have the means to care for and on and on. Because God is omniscient, meaning He knows everything all the time, He can see further down the road in our lives than we can, so He won't always allow things to happen the way we want it to.

Being able to respect the omniscience of God is VITAL in order to mature in becoming a worshiper. A lot of times, we think we know what we want, but God has to intervene in order to show us we really don't. So He may stop a promotion from happening (because He knows the person you would have to report to would be a nightmare to work for), or He may allow your car to not start (because there was a wreck a few blocks from your house that you could've been involved in), or He won't allow you to win a million dollars tomorrow (because you would be broke again in a month). We don't always agree or understand His decisions for our lives, but **WE DO KNOW** that He deserves the respect from us as our Creator to trust His sovereignty to make those decisions.

*Honor:

Webster's II Riverside Dictionary's definition is this: Honor: respect. *Recognition or distinction. Privilege. Reputation. A source or cause of credit To accept as valid.*

WOW! This is what the Word says about Honor:

"He who brings an offering of praise and thanksgiving honors and glorifies Me; and he who orders his way aright [who prepares the way that I may show him], to him I will demonstrate the salvation of God." **Psalm 50:23 (AMP Version)**

"For You, O God, have heard my vows; You have given me the heritage of those who fear, revere, and honor Your name." **Psalm 61:5 (AMP Version)**

"Sing forth the honor and glory of His name; make His praise glorious!" **Psalm 66:2 (AMP Version)**

*"My mouth shall be filled with Your praise and with Your **honor** all the day."*
Psalm 71:8 (AMP Version)

For those that are married, more than likely, part of the marital vows you took on your wedding day included the verbiage: *"...to love, honor and cherish..."* What that means in its essence is how we treat our spouse should surpass how anyone else is treated in our lives. It doesn't mean treat everyone else disrespectfully except your spouse. What it means is **ABOVE ALL ELSE**, treat your spouse with "special privileges." SERIOUSLY! Your spouse should be able to get things done, go places and get the attention that just anybody else should NOT be able to get! You honor your spouse when you listen to their concerns, problems, celebrate them, remember important dates, share your finances, raise your children together jointly, it shows the world the place that person has in your life.

When we HONOR God, we show the world the value and priority we place on our relationship with Him by showing the love of Christ to others, by the extension of ministry be it feeding the hungry, providing clothes and/or shelter for the homeless, visiting the prisons, dropping off hot meals to the elderly; our actions show our honor through our living. In the process of showing that we care toward others, we honor God in the process. You can't be in TRUE ministry and are not in some way showing the love of Christ to others; the two go hand in hand.

CHAPTER 2

NOTES

CHAPTER 3

WHO HAS THE ABILITY TO WORSHIP?

According to the Word, only those who have a personal relationship with the Lord daily, truly understand the essence and ministry of worship. While everyone has the ability to "praise" (let everything that hath breath...) only those who really have relationship with the Father can purely offer, understand or enter into true worship. Worship is considered intercourse with God, so there is no place for sin or contamination where He resides. He demands purity of heart and spirit in His presence. No flesh shall ever glory in His presence.

This is the number #1 thing to know, understand and remember as a worshiper: *"God is a Spirit: and they that worship him must worship him in spirit and in truth."* **John 4:24**

God is telling us in this scripture that He is purposefully looking for a CERTAIN type of worshiper. He's giving the characteristics of that person in this verse. If you read John 3:3-8 you will find that Jesus was clarifying to the Pharisee Nicodemus WHO could actually commune with the Spirit of God. (Genuine worship is created and made exclusive to the person whose Spirit is BORN AGAIN by the Holy Spirit). Jesus' response to Nicodemus in the 3rd verse was: *"... Verily, verily, I say unto thee, except a man be born again, he cannot see the kingdom of God."* What Jesus was saying was, unless you are RENEWED from above, you'll never UNDERSTAND nor EXPERIENCE the Kingdom of God. Your mind has to change and be elevated in order to "get it!" You can't be a worshiper and be carnal in your actions, thinking or understanding of who HE IS; you can ONLY worship Him in spirit and in truth.

HEART CHECK!

Contrary to what many may or may not believe, we are now living in a time where just attending church services on a weekly or regular basis is not enough! For a lot of the challenges we face and are experiencing, it will require a deeper commitment of faith in order to spiritually understand what is going on around us. All it takes is watching the news (especially on the cable channels) for one day. It would appear the whole world is falling apart. For the believer however, we MUST know that all is not lost and that there is Someone much more powerful than us who is ultimately in charge of our destinies and our lives. When we worship God, it's imperative to let Him know that we understand His awesomeness to the degree that we may not have all the answers to what's going on around us but **HE SURE DOES!!** The building of our faith in God is what allows us NOT to worry about tomorrow, or who is (or is not) in public office, because God Himself is still on the Throne; meaning He is still the God that is in charge!

Here are some additional background scriptures to help you know what type of worshiper God longs for:

"For all those things hath mine hand made, and all those things have been, saith the LORD: but to this man will I look, even to him that is poor and of a contrite spirit, and trembleth at my word." **_Isaiah 66:2_**

3"Who shall ascend into the hill of the LORD? or who shall stand in his holy place?

4He that hath clean hands, and a pure heart; who hath not lifted up his soul unto vanity, nor sworn deceitfully.

5He shall receive the blessing from the LORD, and righteousness from the God of his salvation.

6This is the generation of them that seek him, that seek thy face, O Jacob." Selah.
Psalm 24:3-6

"And as for me, thou upholdest me in mine integrity, and settest me before thy face for ever." **Psalm 41:12**

"He that worketh deceit shall not dwell within my house: he that telleth lies shall not tarry in my sight." **Psalm 101:7**

Genuine worship is based and revealed in TRUTH, not what you think or your opinion. Whatever God says is **TRUE WORSHIP**, just is and it's not a secret; it can all be found in His Word.

You will find at the end of many of the Psalms, the word *"selah"* appears. The word Selah is mentioned 73 times in the Book of Psalms and only one time in the Book of Habbakuk. Although the exact meaning of the word isn't known, in general, the word Selah simply means to "think about this or to ponder." Usually something profound is being spoken in that scripture that requires some additional thought, to pause, ponder or meditate on. It's usually an indication that we need to reflect on something that was just stated in that scripture.

Now let's begin to look at the very beginnings of where worship came from as far as the setup or practices that they used back in Biblical times. By reviewing the following, this may help you to understand where some of our own modern day worship practices came from and why some of them are no longer used or are necessary for the way we worship today.

OLD TESTAMENT WORSHIP PRACTICES:

According to the Bible, one of the FIRST acts of worship that was recorded in the Old Testament was when Abraham was ready to slay his own son Isaac just because God asked him to offer him as a sacrifice.

Although God saved Isaac from death and never really intended to have him killed by providing a ram in the bush to die in his stead, it was proven that although Abraham loved his son that he waited so long to have with Sarah his wife, He loved God even more.

You may read about this story further in **Genesis 22nd Chapter**; with emphasis on **Verse 5).**

OLD TESTAMENT SACRIFICES

In the Old Testament, sacrifices were less than perfect, but always required something to die in another's place to justify a wrong. So oftentimes a dove, a lamb, a ram, were utilized in place of a person. Rest assured, something was going to have to die in the stead of someone or something else's wrong doing. Sacrifices during these times usually ended up being the best that someone had of something: their best lamb, their best cow. It had to be something of **VALUE** that was being sacrificed.

Let's review the way the temple for worship use to be setup in the Old Testament. You may start reading the actual scriptures from where I draw this beginning with the 25th Chapter of Exodus.

A BRIEF HISTORY LESSON ON OLD TESTAMENT WORSHIP
Exodus 25th Chapter

The Tabernacle in Biblical times was designed by God and constructed under the leadership of Moses by the children of Israel. It consisted of the following:

a.   **The Sacred Tent:** A place of worship where the presence of God would dwell. The tent served as a place for worship where God would receive their sacrifices, gifts and offerings, worship and hear their prayers. It was a place that demanded honor and reverence. Our modern day "tent" is what we call our church buildings or where we attend to worship every week.

The Sanctuary itself is where most of the worship goes forth and would be likened unto the Sacred Tent of the Old Testament.

b.   **The Altar:** Made from wood and covered with bronze. All of the utensils used with the altar were made of bronze (pans, shovels, basins, fire pans). When coming into God's presence, you approached the altar bringing a sacrifice for sin or a thanksgiving offering. Although today we don't sacrifice animals and the like anymore, we do offer our sacrifices in our giving through our financial substance (money), time, talents and care we show toward our Pastors or overseers of our ministries. Our modern day altar is usually at the front of the church where the leadership usually conducts services from and is usually open to those needing or requiring prayer or desiring to be forgiven for sins and our giving during offertory.

c.   **The Laver:** The laver was a washing bowl used for cleansing purposes. It was a water-filled basin for the Levites and Priests to wash their hands and feet before entering the Temple in the wilderness so they could clean themselves before going on duty. Water was always the cleansing agent physically and spiritually. The laver was also made of bronze and located between the altar and the Tabernacle. Today we use the water of baptism as an outward sign of the cleansing or washing of our sins and coming into our new person or being "born again" in Christ. The practice of the baptism also symbolizes us going down in the water as in "death" of the old life and being brought up out of the water as Christ rose from the dead, embracing a NEW life in Him.

d.   **The Oil:** Consisted of pure myrrh, sweet smelling cinnamon, aromatic cane, cassia and olive oil. This recipe of how to prepare it came straight from God to Moses.

This qualified as a sacred Anointing oil. Moses was also instructed to anoint the Tabernacle itself, the Ark, the table and furnishings, the lamp stand, all the utensils, the laver, and its pedestal. All of this anointing was to signify that they had been consecrated to God as holy. Moses also used this same recipe of anointing oil to anoint Aaron and his sons, consecrating them as holy priests to serve God. Many churches, (not all) still anoint people with oil before praying for them or over them. It is used solely as an outward tool and show of faith that God will hear and answer our prayers.

e.   **The Incense:** Burning incense honored God and also was utilized as part of a ritual to cleanse people of their sins. The recipe for incense consisted of sweet spices, stacte, galbanium and pure frankincense in equal amounts. A perfumer had to blend the fragrances with salt and a pure and holy incense. This in and of itself was considered an act of worship. The high priest on the day of atonement carried a smoking censer in front of him. The thick smoke served as a shield before the presence of God on the mercy seat. The smoke itself became a symbol of prayers ascending to God. There are still some churches (especially in Catholicism) that use this practice, but most modern day church ministries do not as a normal practice.

f.   **The Oil and Incense:** These items were holy unto the Lord for his specific place of worship and were not allowed to be used for ordinary people or personal agendas. The penalty of violating these requirements....**death!**

A STUDY ON THE ARK OF THE COVENANT

Scripture Reference: II Samuel 6th Chapter:

The Ark: The Ark of the Covenant represented the presence of God. It was a wood-based chest with **pure gold** inside and out.

Four gold rings fastened to each corner; two long poles passed through, enabling the Ark to be carried by holding the poles. The Ark of the Covenant carried the tablets of stone that God gave to Moses on Mt. Sinai as recorded in the book of Exodus Chapter 20. The finger of God Himself wrote the laws of His covenant on these tablets of stone. The stones expressed God's desire for the Children of Israel's behavior toward Him and each other. The Ark of the Covenant was a mutual agreement between Him and His chosen people. Since covenants are Holy, this made the Ark itself Holy. Later, other items began to be placed inside of the Ark: a golden jar of manna, a piece of Aaron's rod and Moses' full Book of the Law. The lid of the Ark was covered in pure gold and called the **Mercy Seat.** This is where the Children of Israel could receive a pardon/forgiveness for their sins. At each end of the Mercy Seat, two Cherubims (angels) faced one another.

The Location of the Ark: The Ark was strategically placed in the Tabernacle. It was kept inside of the innermost part of the "most holy place" called the "Holy of Holies." Only the High Priest (not any priest) could enter this part of the Tabernacle and only one time per year! This annual event has become known in our day as Yom Kippur or The Day of Atonement. The Mercy Seat would be sprinkled seven times with blood and was the appointed time for the high priest to enter the Holy of Holies to receive mercy and forgiveness for the sins of all the people. The High Priest had bells around the bottom of his robe and a rope around his waist in case when he entered the Holy of Holies; if he dropped dead, they could drag him out! That meant, even though the High Priest was going in on behalf of the people, if his life wasn't right (holy) going in, he might not make it out **ALIVE himself!**

The Holy of Holies: In the Tabernacle in front of the Veil of Holies, stood the **Table of Showbread**. It consisted of 12 loaves of showbread (representing the tribes of Judah). On the Sabbath, the priests entered the Tabernacle, ate the loaves and replaced them with fresh ones. The word showbread meant: **"Bread of the Presence."** There were also two (2) golden objects before the veil to the Holy of Holies. The first being similar to the **Table Of Showbread** and the second being the **Menorah**. The Menorah (or large lamp stand like a candleholder) resembled the symbol for the tree of life. It consisted of seven oil cups at the top. The burning lamps represented the presence of God. These were made of pure gold, **which was a requirement.** Some of the other furnishings were just gold plated. The olive oil was special made and burned in the seven oil cups at the top of the Menorah.

THE PROTECTORS OF THE TABERNACLE

According to 1 Chronicles 23rd Chapter, the designated protectors of the Tabernacle were the sons from the Tribe of Levi (the priestly ones) or The Levites. The duties were divided among the tribe. One of Aaron's sons, Ithamar was in charge of supervising the word of God's dwelling place.

THE DANGERS OF DISRESPECTING THE PRESENCE OF GOD

If you're not familiar with what the Ark of the Covenant is in the Old Testament, you *may* remember one of my FAVORITE movies of all times: **"Raiders of the Lost Ark"** which starred Harrison Ford (the VERY FIRST movie in the series). His character, Indiana Jones was an archaeologist who was looking for the Ark of the Covenant in order to protect it, its contents and its legacy from bureaucratic government archaeologists...who were ALSO looking for the Ark themselves but of course, with a different motive....**TO GET RICH, BECOME FAMOUS and GAIN NOTORIETY!**

44

While the government's archaeologists' were looking for the Ark strictly for personal gain, Indiana Jones was looking for it in order to preserve what it stood for. He understood the purpose of this ancient piece of Biblical history as well as what would happen if it got into the wrong hands! Needless to say at the end of the movie when the government's paid archaeologists ended up with it, they were ALL destroyed...WHY? Because they didn't understand the Ark's significance, its history and in the process, disrespected the presence of God and what the Ark represented by the way they handled it just like the people who came in contact with it during the days of the Old Testament. See, if they had known what Indiana Jones knew, maybe they would've survived the wrath of God that mishandling His presence brought upon them by the end of the movie!

Even after all of these centuries of it being lost, when they found it, **THE REQUIREMENTS** of how we were to treat it **NEVER CHANGED!** God was STILL demanding respect and reverence! If you've never watched this movie in part or at all, I HIGHLY recommend you see it! Go rent it, buy it on DVD or order it on one of your cable network movie channels...get your popcorn ready and enjoy the movie!!

Why did I bring up this movie? Because the movie "Raiders of the Lost Ark" was a "what if?" fictional scenario of what MIGHT happen if the Ark of the Covenant was found in the 21st Century by some greedy zealots! The FACT is that the Ark of the Covenant is a REAL Biblical artifact that really did exist and has major significance as to how worship ties into our Biblical history.

In 1 Samuel 5th Chapter, it accounts for the existence of the Ark of the Covenant. The Ark was **NO JOKE and not to be played with!** It contained the manifested presence of God inside of it.

If you didn't understand that, your life was automatically in DANGER! In fact, I refer to this time period as **"the Ark on Tour"**. The Ark went from country to country, from Ebenezer to Ashdod and beyond. As we continue to study this period, we discover the Ark kept getting into the hands of people who did not understand nor realize what they had in their possession, so they didn't know HOW to treat it. Every time one country ended up with it and people began getting killed, they wanted to send it off somewhere else for fear of losing their own lives. But in 2nd Samuel the 6th Chapter, it finally came to rest inside of the House of a Godly man named Obed-dom (a Gittite). See, King David had witnessed for himself the deaths of men such as Uzzah whose lives had been taken by misuse of the Ark. Uzzah and the sons of Abinadab put the Ark of the Covenant on a "new" cart and brought it out of the house of Abinadab to take it to the threshing floor of Nacon. While in transit, the animals toting the cart hit a bump, and Uzzah put out his hands to keep the Ark from falling off the cart, and immediately **HE WAS KILLED** instantly! Why? You're probably thinking? All he did was try to keep the Ark from falling off the cart! ...because he simply TOUCHED the Ark; ANYBODY that touched the Ark and didn't have permission to or know what they were doing, the penalty was this simple....**DEATH!**

So even King David, architect of praise and worship, was afraid of the Ark and didn't want to bring it in to the City of David just yet...BUT, he did agree to send it to the House of Obed-edom until he decided what he wanted to do with it himself. Now you can imagine that Obed-e-dom's neighbors were probably terrified that he had this *"thing"* in his house! They probably were scared for his life, the life of his family, and probably THEIR OWN because he took possession of it. But what they DIDN'T know, is that Obed-e-dom was a **WORSHIPER!**

He loved God and made ROOM for the Ark of the Covenant to stay in his house. For him, it was AN HONOR to have the presence of God residing where he and his family lived. The Ark remained there for three months, according to the Word of God. **EVERYTHING IN HIS HOUSE AND LIFE PROSPERED the entire time it was in his possession!** Since Obed-e-dom and his family weren't dead yet from the Ark literally being in his house, I'm sure everyone was wondering... *"what in the world is Obed-e-dom doing that the rest of those that died before him DIDN'T do?...or what does HE KNOW that we don't know concerning the Ark of the Covenant?"*

Soon word got back to King David that Obed-e-dom and his family were **STILL ALIVE** and not only alive but **PROSPERING** with the Ark in their house! God had blessed the House of Obed-e-dom which gave King David **GREAT FAITH** that it was alright (safe) for him to bring the Ark back into the City of David!

What did King David learn from Obed-e-dom? That when you make room for God's presence, your life will PROSPER! Obed-e-dom didn't just get to know God when the Ark arrived....**HE ALREADY HAD A RELATIONSHIP WITH GOD** by the time the offer for him to keep the Ark came from King David. He welcomed God's presence....that's what worship is; making room for God's presence to be welcomed in our lives. King David learned that he didn't have to FEAR the Ark, but make room and welcomed it back to its rightful place: **The City of David.** Ever hear the story of David *"dancing out of his clothes?"* Well this is EXACTLY when it happened, when King David prepared a celebration to welcome the Ark of the Covenant back into the city.

David had prepared a place for the Ark to reside inside the tent BEFORE it arrived; again he was mimicking what Obed-e-dom did, he made room or a dwelling place for the Ark!

THE OLD ORDER OF WORSHIP – WE'VE BEEN DELIVERED!

While there are still requirements, even today, in order to come into the presence of the Lord, we have been delivered from having the High Priest of old to go before the Lord on our behalf so we could acquire forgiveness. The veil has been ripped and we have access ourselves to enter into the Holy of Holies which is still God's dwelling place!

The difference now is that the presence of the Ark of the Covenant doesn't carry the weight it used to because it isn't needed since God has changed His place of residence and His manifestation in the earth realm. Jesus LIVES and His presence now resides **inside of us**! Jesus IS our sacrifice and our mediator! He is now our High Priest. He's so big of a God, He could NEVER just reside in one person. No one person could ever hold ALL of the Anointing...that's why so many of God's people carry such a diversity of His gifts, talents and Anointing on their lives. That's why it's important for all people to recognize that his/her body are the Temple of God and it is to be consecrated before Him.

CHAPTER 3

NOTES

CHAPTER 4

WORSHIP - A DEEPER UNDERSTANDING

The Biblical Order of Worship – The Requirements

"But the hour cometh, and now is, when the true worshippers shall worship the Father in spirit and in truth: for the Father seeketh such to worship him. ." John 4:23

"God is a Spirit: and they that worship him must worship him in spirit and in truth." John 4:24

The above are two scriptures that specifically inform us of what God is looking for through those that claim to worship Him. Notice how emphatic He is on the characteristics of "spirit and in truth." This suggests to me that these qualities ARE NOT negotiable.

*Worshiping God in spirit and truth are **REQUIREMENTS**…not a suggestion.

*Worship requires discipline, effort and practice; we must PRACTICE His presence in our daily lives.

*Worshipers **MUST** know the Word of God in order to effectively LEAD a worship service. Being an exhorter to the people is part of your job!

*Worship is a **PRIVILEGE** and is reserved for those who are willing to qualify to get into His presence.

*Worship requires purified **ATTITUDES, PRIORITIES** and **MOTIVES**.

*Worshipers are **Anointed by God ONLY!** Your Pastor can only **appoint** a worship leader. Don't confuse your Anointing with your Appointment or Assignment. <u>**NO ONE CAN OPERATE UNDER AN ANOINTING THEY DON'T HAVE!**</u>

*Worshipers **NEVER** seek glory for themselves but always point the attention to the One worthy of the glory!

*Worshipers learn to MAINTAIN the glory on them; they are peculiar people!

HEART CHECK!

<u>JESUS! OUR DELIVERER OF THE OLD ORDER OF WORSHIP</u>

You, as a worshiper, should be OVERJOYED that we no longer have to submit to the Mosaic law of the blood sacrifices! Our covenant now is made of GRACE due to the covenant David made with God. Our access to God is modeled after David's Tabernacle rather than Moses' which is the model we discussed out of Exodus 25-30th Chapters. David's worship model (found in 1 Chronicles 22-26th Chapters) is VERY distinguished from Moses mainly because of the Order of worship and the allowance of FREE ACCESS into the presence of God, which is what the Ark contained. The restoration of David's Tabernacle was so that ALL of mankind may desire to seek God through the avenue of worship. Davidic worship, which we will discuss a little later, was intended to be modeled for the believer's of the New Covenant.

Jesus was made the sacrifice of **ALL MANKIND** so that we may now come boldly to the throne of Grace for ourselves instead of needing a priest to do it on our behalf. Jesus Himself desires a personal relationship with you in order to establish the relationship you should have with Him the rest of your life. He's **PERSONAL.** He's hands on. He's reliable and He's made Himself available to EACH of us through DIRECT relationship. Thank God that the way has been made through **Jesus Christ our Redeemer!**

<u>YOU CAN'T WORSHIP A GOD YOU DON'T KNOW FOR YOURSELF!</u>

Part of being able to worship God is to be able to recognize who He is; that is, you must learn to identify Him at work in our own daily life, situations and circumstances. That is why it is a **REQUIREMENT** that the righteous have to suffer sometimes. How else will you be able to know that it was ONLY GOD that delivered you? God is so big and so vast, there is no one name to handle all of what or who He is! These are <u>some</u> (and He has many) of the Biblical names of God; these Names alone are reason enough to worship Him!

See if you can recognize God or remember Him manifesting Himself in your own life in one of these capacities:

Yahweh-Jehovah   **The Lord**
                         The God Who ALWAYS IS
                         The Self-Sufficient God
                         The Real God
                         The Unchangeable God
                         The Self-Fulfilled God

Deut. 6:4

Daniel 9:14

Exodus 3:14

Psalm 25:11

Psalm 31:3

Psalm 107:13

Jehovah-Jireh   **The Lord God who provides our needs!**

The God of Provision

Reference Scripture:

Genesis 22:14

Jehovah-Elohim   **The Lord IS God!**

A God Who is Worthy of Worship

Reference Scriptures:

Genesis 1:1

Genesis 17:7

Jeremiah 31:33

Jehovah-Elyon   **The Most High God! (Our High Priest)**

The Possessor of Heaven and Earth

The Deliverer

The God Who is Greater

Reference Scripture:

Deut. 26:19

El-Shaddai   **The Almighty, All Sufficient God!**

The God of Greatness

<u>Reference Scriptures</u>:

Genesis 49:24

Psalm 132:2, 5

Jehovah-Ropheka   **The Lord our Healer!**
Or Rapha or Rophe'

<u>Reference Scripture:</u>

Exodus 15:26

Jehovah-Tsidqenu   **The Lord our Righteousness!**
Or Tsidkenu

<u>Reference Scriptures:</u>

Jeremiah 33:16

2 Corin. 5:21

Jehovah-Shalom   **The God of my Peace!**

The Lord IS Peace

The Lord Who Comforts In the Midst of

Confusion

<u>Reference Scripture:</u>

Judges 6:24

Jehovah-Shammah   **The God that is ALWAYS present!**

The Lord Will Be There With Us

The Lord Is Here Now!

The Lord Is Present in Trouble

(Jehovah-Shammah cont'd)

The Lord Is Present in Loneliness

The Lord Is Present in Persecution

Reference Scriptures:

Ezekiel 44:1-4

Ezekiel 48:35

Jehovah Nissi   **The God who Reigns in Victory!**

The Lord My Banner

The Lord that Fights For You

Reference Scripture:

Exodus 17:15

Jehovah-Tsebaoth   **The Lord of Hosts**

Or Sabaoth   I Am That I Am

The Lord Who Is A Warrior

The Lord of Armies

The Lord Who Judges Nations

The Lord Our Captain

Reference Scriptures:

Isaiah 1:24

Psalm 46:7

Adonai   **Lord**

Reference Scriptures:

Genesis 15:2

Judges 6:15

El Eloah   God, Mighty, Strong and Prominent

Reference Scriptures:

Genesis 7:1

Genesis 31:29

Numbers 23:19

Deut. 5:9

Nehemiah 9:31

Isaiah 9:6

Yahweh M'Kaddesh   **The Lord Who Sanctifies**

The Lord Who Makes Holy

Reference Scriptures:

Leviticus 20:8

Ezekiel 37:28

Yahweh Rohi   **The Lord Our Shepherd**

Reference Scritpure:

Psalm 23:1

El Roi   **The God of Seeing**

Reference Scriptures:

Genesis 6:13

Genesis 16:1-14

El Olam   **The Everlasting God**

Reference Scripture:

Psalm 90:1-3

El Gibhor   **The Mighty God**

Reference Scriptures:

Isaiah 9:6

Revelations 19:15

Regardless, we serve an awfully **BIG GOD!** These are just a few Names that God is known for throughout scripture....can you find **OTHERS** that I didn't list? **STUDY** to shew thyself approved...

CHAPTER 4

NOTES

CHAPTER 5

UNDERSTANDING THE WAR BETWEEN GOD AND satan
"Calling All Worship Warriors!"

As I stated in my other book: **PRAISE – The Foundation for Servants of the Worship Arts Ministry**, which is the complementary read to this book, the origins as far as we know of where music was first introduced to us in the Bible happened in Heaven when satan actually lived there and was previously known as the angelic being, lucifer. He was also known as **"The Anointed Cherub."**

Why do I bring this up again? Because I think it's important for those that are reading this book to understand WHY worship is of such value in this spiritual war that has been going on between God and satan and to help us recognize some of the attributes, personalities and characteristics of lucifer that exist and are often in operation in our churches and music departments. It's actually **WORSHIP** that is the center of all this controversy. Do you really think they would've been engaged in all of this WAR over the ministry of worship if it wasn't something about it that was appealing, valuable, necessary and powerful? **WORSHIP CHANGES THINGS!** This whole war between God and satan that is going on will eventually, when all is said and done, be won through the ministry of worship.

How do I know this? Let's look at the record. The events of lucifer having residency in Heaven must have taken place **BEFORE** the fall of Adam and Eve since satan was already living on earth and shows up in the book of Genesis in the Garden of Eden as a snake. Sin didn't occur until Adam and Eve's disobedience to God took place in the Garden of Eden and they were tempted by the snake (satan) to eat of the forbidden fruit.

If satan was on earth during Adam and Eve's time, then lucifer (who is the same being in heavenly form) existed **PRIOR** to his being booted out of Heaven and satan gaining access in the earth realm.

In God's quest to cleanse Heaven of satan and his pride that rose up against Him, He also banished about 2/3 of the angels that were stupid enough to get in behind satan's attempt to "overthrow" Heaven and its Leadership.

In the book of Ezekiel the 28th Chapter, is where we find lucifer in Heaven. Since God is actually seated in the Throne Room, we see that lucifer must have had access to this very area. Now according to these scriptures, lucifer was in charge of leading the angels in worship.

When God created him, he was THE MOST beautiful angel in the Heavens and created with great purpose: to give God glory through worship and music. The instruments that would be used to glorify God were built into lucifer's being, so in essence **HE WAS** the music department all by himself! The 14th verse of Ezekiel's 28th Chapter declares:

> 13. *Son of man, take up a lamentation upon the king of Tyrus, and say unto him, Thus saith the Lord GOD; Thou sealest up the sum, full of wisdom, and perfect in beauty.*
>
> 14. *Thou hast been in Eden the garden of God; every precious stone was they covering, the sardius, topaz and the diamond, the beryl, the onyx, and the jasper, the sapphire, the emerald and the carbuncle, and gold: the workmanship of they tabrets and of they pipes was prepared in thee in the day that thou was created.*

Now, what's not exactly known is **WHEN** lucifer decided he no longer wanted to be leading worship but to BE the one that IS worshiped! This is where we find the luciferic spirit of pride coming into play and lucifer was full of it.

Arrogance had obviously set in by this time. It is imperative that we understand that although satan got kicked out of Heaven, God **DID NOT** dismantle him nor the ability He gave him. Music was still all inside of his being. Even the Bible declares in Romans 11:29: *"For the gifts and calling of God are without repentance."* What exactly does that mean Doris?

Well, basically God won't necessarily recall a gift(s) because people are ungrateful, full of pride and live unholy. Eventually, the very gift He allowed them to have will destroy them if they aren't careful. Let's look at it this way. I'm sure we all know some arrogant singers, musicians, songwriters, and so on that have exceptional gifts and musical abilities to the degree that it has gone to their heads and filled these individuals up with deadly pride in and out of the church. Many of them (not all) aren't living Godly lives and aren't trying to but are serving in many of our churches. Yet God has not withdrawn many of their gifts from them because of it. A lot of times, God has allowed those very people to KEEP their gift and they ran it into the ground where they dug their own grave with it.....sad but true. So just because you possess a gift that may be above average, if you aren't representing God in a favorable light, it means nothing and carries little to no weight in the Kingdom. Matthew 16:26 states: *"For what is a man profited, if he shall gain the whole world, and lose his own soul? Or what shall a man give in exchange for his soul?"*

This is **POWERFUL** because we've all witnessed so many of our secular artists who had phenomenal talents, the whole world seemed to love them, they had all the money and worldly possessions anybody could EVER want, all the connections, all the big name friends, big cars, big houses, but they died overdosing on drugs, depression, broke due to mismanagement of their own money, not able to control their flesh, unhappy, etc. It's truly sad when you allow the luciferic spirit to deceive you into TOTALLY believing that your gift and talents are above and beyond everybody else and **ARE ENOUGH** to keep you in life. It is ALWAYS appropriate to acknowledge where your gift(s) come from. I am by **NO MEANS** suggesting that everyone who sings or plays an instrument should end up singing Gospel. I do however, feel a great deal of respect for secular artists who can give God credit, respect or recognition by acknowledging Him for their gifts and music abilities; ESPECIALLY when they can do it on a large platform to honor the One who graced them with the talent. Gifts without any accountability for them are dangerous. Your soul is PRICELESS and will one day end up in one realm or another; Heaven or Hell. It's your choice and you make that decision by how you live your life out down here on earth.

So lucifer, was kicked out of Heaven with his magnificence and ability to make music still in tact. It should now be clearer to see and understand why so much of our music today is so tainted and foul. It's satan's way of getting back at God (so to speak) for demoting him. So much so, that he's gotten bold enough to try and taint the very music we utilize to give God glory from. Talk about **BOLD!**

Today, our churches are experiencing huge personnel and personality issues with musicians who prostitute their gifts and on the other hand, some pastors who are in return trying to manipulate our minstrels in order to get what they want.

A lot of church leadership facilitators don't feel those that serve in music ministry should EVER be compensated monetarily, but I don't agree with that. The Bible teaches us in Luke 10:7: *"And in the same house remain, eating and drinking such things as they give: for the labourer is worthy of his hire. Go not from house to house."* So clearly we that serve the Body of Christ diligently and have the call of God on our lives to work in His vineyard in other capacities other than just Pastoring, are worthy of our time, efforts, talents, education, expertise and abilities to be compensated for our work and contributions.

On the other hand, we as laborers and Kingdom servants should **IN RETURN** be committed to the cause of Christ and to the vision of the House we serve. Even if you are planted there for a season, respecting and obeying the man or woman of God's vision for their House (church) should be first and foremost; we should ALWAYS follow their lead, not come in with our own agenda and motives.

However, many musicians while gifted have no idea, background or understanding of the ability the Lord has given them or entrusted them with. Therefore, they go from church to church or artist to artist, whomever is the **HIGHEST BIDDER** for their talents but they are NEVER connected or committed to **ANYTHING.** The only thing they care about is *"how much money am I going to make?"* It's so bad that a LOT of these musicians even refer to their playing for church ministries as **"gigs"** which is a secular term the world uses to refer to *"an engagement."* As a servant of the worship arts ministry, it hurts my heart to even hear musicians use that term in relation to what they are doing in the House of God or in the Kingdom. Referring to playing for any church or artist as a "gig" is so demeaning and disrespectful (in my opinion).

Most do not realize that the very behavior of what they are exhibiting is no worse than what the world calls **prostitution.** That didn't come from me, it came from the Word of God. The only difference is the Bible calls those that carry that spirit to go to the highest bidder, **HIRELINGS!**

This is what the Word has to say about those that carry or operate under a "hireling" spirit in John 10:12:13:

"But he that is an hireling, and not the shepherd, whose own sheep are not, seeth the wolf coming, and leaveth the sheep, and fleeth: and the wolf catcheth them, and scattereth the sheep.

The hireling fleeth, because his is an hireling and careth not for the sheep."

The Word is telling us, when you **ARE NOT** the Shepherd (Pastor or Overseer) and just basically want your "pay" for what you do, you don't care or connect to what happens in the house OR to its people. You don't connect to the House's (church) vision, the Pastor's Leadership nor the congregations' needs as it pertains to worship. The attitude usually ends up being from a floating or "gigging" musician's perspective, *"just tell me what songs to play, what key is it in and give me my money."* It's a pimp spirit straight from lucifer that is desperately trying to overtake and destroy our Houses of Worship!

HEART CHECK!

Once satan was banished from Heaven, the war between he and God was on! He (satan) probably has the longest grudge of anybody known to humanity, because he still carries it against God and all who God has ordained to replace him....**US!**

I guess you could view it like this; satan's "beef" is with God but is also (kind of with us) as well. Why? Because God has now given us the role in the earth realm that satan use to have in Heavenly realm. We are the ones called to worship God in the beauty of holiness; satan will NEVER have the opportunity to regain his position ever again because God has now entrusted that to us.

When we speak of war, we're talking about two entities that are usually in opposition to each other. In this case, it's God and satan himself. Our worship should flow upward (vertically), focused, meaning ascending toward the God of Creation. Worship is reserved for Him, which is the way He created it to be. The "war" part comes in when you consider what we are doing. When we think of war we start to think about weapons, someone or something being a threat to us, overcoming or conquering a foe, and so on. There are different types and phases to our worship; in Old Testament times, the way they strategized how to win wars was even a form of worship. When they won their battles or wars, they gave praises to God for their victories which were also a form of worship. They would take the spoils of those they overthrew and give offerings unto the Lord with them, which was a form of worship. In actuality, the war and the worship were actually working together in these instances, although often war is viewed quite separate from our worship altogether.

So what are you saying Doris? Well, I think God wants us to view it this way as well. I believe we are approaching the time that God wants to transform our thinking, our hearts and our attitudes regarding worship. Many have been taught to believe it's just about the songs or the singing, the dance ministry, and so on and that is all a part of it....outwardly. But by us living in the last days (and we are), we will need to tighten up our view of what is actually happening.

God has given us an awesome authority over spiritual darkness and wickedness (evil). We are reminded in 2 Corinthians 2:4:

> 4. *For the weapons of our warfare are not carnal, but mighty through God to the pulling down of strong holds.*
> 5. *Casting down imaginations, and every high thing that exalteth itself against the knowledge of God, and bringing into captivity every thought to the obedience of Christ;*

Just as in the Old Testament times, almost anything they did in the Temple was regarded to some degree as "worship." From who lit the candles, to who cleaned the Temple and locked it up for the night. So it is today; we must allow our idea of what worship is for US, to line up with what God says our worship is or should be.

God is now releasing a sound from Heaven that only those with spiritual ears to hear will be able to respond to. This sound is engaging us to war on a higher spiritual level. He is assembling his last days **Worship Warriors!** Those that will not only hear but LIVE and OBEY his Word. Being a part of this particular army is a given if you are a believer in Jesus Christ; you are already enrolled!

We need to stop thinking that the work of ministry or the responsibility of worship is only for the Pastor, the Bishop, our Music Ministry or our Leaders in the Body of Christ. Worship is the responsibility of **ANY BELIEVER** who embraces the ministry of Jesus as Savior and Lord and has developed a personal, intimate relationship with the Lord.

If you notice, the devil has created NO ONE and nothing, yet he's bold enough to "seek those he may devour" according to (1 Peter 5:8) and use for his own glory.

This is why you see so many unnecessary shootings against our children, robberies, people selling drugs, embezzlements, prostitution, you name it. If you leave the door open for him to use you, he will automatically enlist you for his purposes.

Now, if God is the Creator of **ALL THINGS**, doesn't He have even MORE of a right to utilize all the people in His possession and everything He has rightfully created to his cause? The call of God is going out and is LOUDER than ever before! We need to live our lives by always being in position and ready for battle. When we speak of God being in the "Throne Room", He is still there and awaits our pure worship to ascend unto Him, offered as a sacrifice from His people. He awaits the worship we release to Him; it should arise as a sweet smelling savour to His nostrils. Everything in our lives should reflect our desire to give Him what He asks of us. Our worship should be more than just the fight, a song, a dance or the playing of instruments but the offering of our worship for the One we fight on behalf of! God seeks to bridge the gap in our warring and our worship by showing us how to do both while He still receives the glory.

We are living in a time where almost anything apparently goes and is being accepted as "right" and "good." We know through God's word that no matter the season, the reason, the age, the year, the decade, nor who is President, who isn't, who serves in Washington and who doesn't....**GOD'S WORD NEVER CHANGES!** Holiness is still right and is GOD'S STANDARD for righteousness. It is up to us as the people of God to be standard bearers according to His word. We can't expect politicians to do it, it's not their job. He left the mandate of righteousness on the earth to be carried out by His people; His representatives.

The Clarion call is being made and we as His own must stand for righteousness by **LIVING** the worship we sing, play our instruments and dance about.

Whenever we speak of winning others to Christ, we must know and understand that we'll never do it without the love of Christ being exemplified. When Christ Himself walked the earth, He was a living testament to the worship He offered Father God everyday. No matter who He may have encountered on the earth, no matter what kind of sin they may have been caught in, or what type of lifestyle they lived, He never condemned them, but won them over through the love He showed them.
If we expect to "war" against the sin we see, we have to LIVE the righteousness that we want them to consider accepting. The lifestyle of worship that undesirable people may witness us living will win them over far quicker than bashing them over the head with scriptures!

Often times we are being watched by those that we have no idea are paying attention to us. I remember a young lady that parked in the same parking garage as I did everyday when we showed up to work. She always looked like she walked in depression, just a heavy spirit over her every time I encountered her. But every morning I would greet her with a smile and say *"Good morning, how are you? Good to see you today!"* Most of the time, she would "half speak" like she didn't want to be bothered, but I continued to speak to her the same way whenever I saw her. This went on for months. Then one morning, I didn't show up for work, I was ill and off for several days, but she didn't see me. When I returned to work after a few days, I saw her again and I gave her my usual greeting: *"Good morning, how are you? Good to see you today!"*

Low and behold...she actually TALKED to me on this morning! She said, "You know I've missed you the last few days and wondered where you were. I know you never knew this, but you are the **ONLY PERSON** that ever speaks to me like I matter on a daily basis. I actually looked forward to you greeting me every morning!" I thanked her and said "Awwww, God bless you, and have a great day." From that day forward, every morning when I saw her, she began to smile, she became friendlier and we even went to lunch a couple of times...why? Because I took the time to speak and say a kind word to her each day. I tried to exemplify the love of Christ toward her.

I found out after the first time we went to lunch, that she didn't know the Lord and had some very bad experiences in her life that led her to believe: *"If there is a God, then why didn't He stop some of the tragedies that I experienced in my life from happening?"* The Lord gave me a platform to minister to her in truth but also in love. She was living with her boyfriend unmarried. After a couple of months, she moved out and got her own apartment. Eventually, I was able to lead her to the Lord but not by banging her over the head with scriptures, but just trying to walk out the WORSHIP that God has placed in me. I "warred" with the enemy for her soul in private, prayed for her everyday until I could see a change; God heard me and He saved her! The victory became God's and hers because she began to see and understand that God really did love and care about her.

I'm calling ALL **Worship Warriors**, it's time to take up your weapons of worship, prayer, praise and use our LIFESTYLES to win the lost for Christ. We have a lot of work to do before His return and this war will be WON through the warfare of worship on behalf of the Father. Let's get ourselves in **POSITION!**

CHAPTER 5

NOTES

CHAPTER 6

PLACING GOD AS THE PRIORITY!

In the Old Testament it was flat dangerous **NOT** to worship God in a proper and acceptable fashion. Worship was a **PRIORITY** to them during that time because they understood the consequences of either **NOT** worshiping God at all or not worshiping Him correctly.

While **I DID** write this book to prayerfully be a VALUABLE resource for you as you study to make sure you understand the ministry of Worship, I want YOU to read the Word (the Bible) FOR YOURSELF so that you can begin to understand what God says, not just what I'm telling you through this publication although ALL of my references come from the Bible. I've provided some scriptures (below) for you to **READ YOUR OWN BIBLE** so you'll have a reason to study!

HEART CHECK!

For a serious worshiper, God being a priority in your life should be without question. Here are some scripture references for you to study and read to help you better understand the importance, value and significance of why worship was so important to them:

a.   Consequences of refusing to worship God caused satan's fall (Isaiah 14:12-14)

b.   Worship was a part of the Old Testament Law (Exodus 20: 1-7, 34:14)

c.   Directives on **Tabernacle Worship** as given to **Moses** (Exodus 25-30 – Chapters)

d.	Directives on **Temple Worship** as given to **David** (1 Chronicles 22-26 – Chapters)
e.	Judgment that fell on Israel for **NOT** Worshiping God (2 Chronicles 7:21-222, 24:18, Jeremiah 16:10-11, 22:8-9)
f.	Those that placed their lives at risk rather than **NOT** Worship God (Daniel 3:10-18, 28, 6:1-28)
g.	Jesus' Choice to Glorify God (John 2:13-17, 8:29, 13:31-32, 17:1)
h.	Worship As A Priority in Early Church Days (Acts 2:42-47)
i.	Worship will continue for all eternity (Revelation 4:10-11, 7:11-12, 11:16-17, 19:4-8)

Worship **SHOULD BE** a logical response of how God's creation reacts toward Him.

(Psalm 95: 6-7) *"O come, let us worship and bow down: let us kneel before the LORD our maker. [7]For he is our God; and we are the people of his pasture, and the sheep of his hand. To day if ye will hear his voice"*

THE PROGRAM FOR WORSHIP

a.	Should consider Substance over style/form (Colossians 2:16-17; Hebrews 10:22; John 4:20-24)
b.	Individual and Corporate Worship (Romans 12:1-2; Luke 10:38-42; Psalm 150:1; Acts 2:42-47; Hebrews 10:25)
c.	Our Inward response and Outward expression (Isaiah 29:13; Psalm 51:15-17; Luke 6:45)

d.   ***Utilizing Worship as a Lifestyle** vs. Compartmenta-
lizing or limiting it to a time or place.
(1 Corinthians 10:31; Colossians 3:17; Hebrews 13:15-16;
John 4:20-24)

e.   Reverencing God and Standing in Awe
(Hebrew 12:28-29)

f.   Not exclusive of Joy (Psalm 100:1-2)

Using the Old Testament as our blueprint, worship is only acceptable when it's done the way God has requested; flowing from a humbled heart and bathed in holiness.

Worship is personal and begins in the personal lives of the individual. Once worshipers come together at church corporately, the worship that is practiced in private will be manifested in public.

Above are some more scripture references for you to **STUDY ON YOUR OWN.** Find out what The Word is saying to you about how you are to CONSIDER Worship as the ministry it is and was designed to be.

*I write a column **"Black Pearls"** that is currently being carried in several National Gospel Publications. My column focuses on helping the Kingdom to **"LIVE THE LIFE"** of praise and worship. What do you mean Doris? Well, I mean we should take some of the real life scenarios we all face daily and find a way to incorporate HOW we may glorify God in those situations. God knows that we encounter many things that aggravate us to NO END; things that may really light up our emotions negatively. However, when we learn to **PRACTICE THE PRESENCE** of God in our lives, it will become habitual to respond to the bricks life throws at us differently.

It doesn't mean we'll always get it right, but the more we practice at it, the better we become. When you live your life as if God is **PHYSICALLY** standing next to you, would you think twice about cussing someone out in public or online on a social media network? Would you think twice before taking more change from the cashier than you were supposed to get, instead of returning the portion that wasn't yours? When you practice the presence of God, it strengthens your **INTEGRITY** as a person and as a Worshiper. You try to watch everything you do and say, or as the old Saints used to say**..."You are Holy Ghost filled!"** It's TRUE! The Holy Spirit helps GOVERN our souls and lives so that we reflect God in our actions. The Holy Ghost will bridle your tongue if you allow Him to. Through my column, I want to encourage my readers by sharing some of my own life experiences and assure them that God wants to gain glory out of EVERYTHING we do. Praise and Worship **IS NOT** just a specified time set aside each week at church to sing songs, jump, and get our "praise on!" That's just a small part of it; it's about LIVING what we're singing about and allowing the presence of God to rule and reign in our daily lives. The Bible declares that people will know **WHO** you are and **WHOSE** you are by the fruit you bare. What kind of fruit does your everyday life bare in comparison to what you are preaching or singing about?

HEART CHECK!

If you would like to check out some of the Gospel Publications that carry my **column "Black Pearls"** feel free to log-on to my Author's Website **www.bpewordpublishing.wix.com/Kingdombooks**, CLICK on the **"Black Pearls" Column** Tab and at the bottom are links to the publications for you to go read and enjoy!

THE PROCESS FOR WORSHIP

a. The offering of spiritual sacrifices (Hebrews 13:15-16; 1 Chronicles 16:29; Romans 12:1; 1 Peter 2:4-5
b. Willfully giving God the glory and praise that is due His Name (Psalm 29:1-2)
c. When we're responding to the truth from preaching, teaching, studying the Word, etc. (Psalm 86:11; John 4:23-24; Colossians 3:16; Nehemiah 8:2-6)
d. When offering of our material resources (Phillipians 4:18)
e. When offering Thanksgiving and Praise unto God (Hebrews 13:15-16)
f. When doing good unto others (Hebrews 13:15-16)
g. When offering of our singing and Zamar Praise (singing w/musical instruments) (Colossians 3:16; Ephesians 5:19; Psalm 150)

Worshipers, I implore you to please remember this:
Music in and of itself IS NOT worship but is only used as a vehicle or tool in offering our worship. The use of Biblical forms of worship (i.e., clapping of your hands, standing, bowing, raising of hands) are forms of how we manifest praise and worship.

In true worship, we must be concerned with what we're giving to God; not what we're getting out of it. **Worship isn't about you;** self is to take a back seat. If you're blessed by the worship experience, that is actually a by-product of what worship will produce but it should not be the motivation for worship. Worship is unselfish in its very essence. **Worship is the desire to access His presence.**

CHAPTER 6

NOTES

CHAPTER 7

THE PRODUCT OF WORSHIP (What Does It Produce?)

God receives honor and glory (Psalm 50:23)
Our hearts are purified and yielded in service to the Lord. (Psalm 24:3-4; Isaiah 6:1-8)

THE DIFFERENCES: OLD TESTAMENT vs.
NEW TESTAMENT WORSHIP

The styles of worship did change from the Old Testament to the New, but God ordained the changes:

Old Testament

*Worship was centered around God's presence and glory in the temple with other specified locations prior to the building of the temple. There were specific times of year the Lord wanted them to worship Him corporately for specific reasons: (Exodus 23: 15 & 16)

> **Feast of Unleavened Bread** – The festival when they ate bread without any yeast baked into it as a reminder of when they were liberated from Egypt.

> **Feast of Harvest** (or The Harvest Festival) - When they were to offer their first fruits of their harvest unto the Lord AND what you sowed in the field.

> **Feast of Ingathering** (or The Festival of Shelters) – An end of the year celebration when they gathered the fruit of their labors.

*Worship involved scheduled and regulated sacrifices and feasts (Leviticus 23 & 25th Chapters)

*Lord's Passover – This was honoring God by eating bread made without yeast. On the first day of the festival, everyone must rest from their labor and worship corporately.

*The Harvest Festival – Where they worshiped God by bringing two loaves of bread made WITH yeast and with four pounds of the finest flour from the FIRST part of your harvest.

*The Festival of Trumpets – This was a time of COMPLETE rest from labor and to offer sacrifices which were to be laid on the altar.

*The Day of Atonement - A solemn day of worship where everyone must fast (go without eating) to show remorse for their sins. All sacrifices were to be burned during this service.

*The Feast of Tabernacles (or The Festival of Shelters) – Where Holy Convocation was held on the first day of the feast. No one was to do laborious work on that day; it was reserved as a day of worship unto the Lord.

Significant importance was placed on method; **HOW** things were carried out. There were certain times of year that God commanded the people of Israel to come together in corporate worship to honor Him for different reasons. The above listed seasons reflect what God ordained for them to do in regards to worshiping Him throughout the year. When reading the scripture texts given above, pay attention to the detail of HOW, WHEN and WHERE God wanted them to hold these festivals; He was very specific. Also notice the importance of the 1st as an offering and the 10th. This is where the word "tithe" comes from and what it references. The first of almost anything during that time was the BEST you could offer God; you never gave God what was left over of anything. They were always careful to make sure their offerings were acceptable unto the Lord by giving their BEST offering and the FIRST (first fruits) of what they had acquired.

New Testament

*Worship is centered around God's presence which can't be contained in a building, place or thing and carried out by His requirement of worshiping Him in **Spirit and in Truth**. (John 4:21-24)

*Worship involves a lifestyle change or incorporates your whole life along with spiritual sacrifices. (Romans 12:1)

*Significant importance is placed on the **"heart."**

WHAT IS "DAVIDIC" WORSHIP?
Worship During the Early Church

What exactly is "Davidic worship" Doris? Well, let's take a look at it. Because David was the "Rescuer" of the Ark of the Covenant and brought it back to its rightful place, (the City of David) to dwell, there was MAJOR rejoicing that took place when this celebration happened! When David was Anointed as King of Israel, literally a NEW ERA was Born. King David is the ONLY person I've found in scripture that God referred to *as "a man after God's own heart."* (1 Samuel 13:14). Surprisingly, with all of David's flaws, God was overall VERY pleased with him.

In order to understand David's passion for worshiping and praising God, you must understand a little about his humble beginnings as recorded in 1 Samuel 16th Chapter. As a little boy, David loved singing and playing instruments. Although, as a child his job was to tend to his fathers' sheep, he did it while worshiping God. No one really knew or understood the Anointing upon David's life until God sent the Prophet Samuel to the house of Jesse (David's father) to anoint him as the forthcoming King. David was the youngest of eight boys but God specifically told Samuel that DAVID was the one He wanted him to Anoint.

David was anointed as a child to play an instrument called a "lyre." It is a part of the harp family. He became extremely skilled at playing it. The reigning King during that time was Saul and he was given over to evil spirits that had taken his right mind. Whenever the evil spirits would torment Saul, they would call David (specifically) to play the lyre, as it was the ONLY thing that could calm King Saul's spirit and mind down. David was a skilled musician; so playing the lyre, had healing elements in the music to calm King Saul's mental instability. King Saul became so fond of David, he made him his armour–bearer and asked his father Jesse, to allow him to come live with him, so David was called to service as a musician. The Anointing of music was upon David even as a child...it was his destiny to become the architect of the worship arts ministry and King of Israel!

When the Ark was returned to the City of David, the Bible declares that David danced harder and wilder than he had EVER danced before. He rejoiced and danced with **ALL HIS MIGHT!** His dancing demonstrated the FREEDOM that he felt after the return of the Ark. He was so free in giving God praise through his dance, that it embarrassed his wife who thought he was acting foolish. What was going on here? David was establishing a **NEW FORM of worship for God's people!** A New Order of worship was being established and ushered in....be FREE to praise God without embarrassment, hinderances or boundaries! David was so serious about HOW God was to be worshiped, he appointed SKILLED musicians and Worship Leaders to worship around the Ark 24/7....YES, day and night their job was to **WORSHIP GOD!**

In David's day, he established the use of various musical instruments and incorporated shouting, bowing, singing, when it came to giving God glory through the use of our beings. He wanted us to use EVERYTHING God gave us in order to give glory back to Him (i.e., clapping, lifting of hands...any of this sound familiar?...previously discussed)

Most of the time, Davidic worship as described in scripture was mainly PROPHETIC in its offering. They would often sing as we would call *"off the cuff"* meaning, spontaneously; the Holy Spirit would inspire songs that were NOT pre-written.

Prophetic worship is an offering that goes forth for what you believe God for even though it may not have happened yet. Looking for the manifestation of it through speaking or singing it into the atmosphere is a powerful process of worship. This type of worship flows from a place of faith; our faith literally has eyes that can see into the eternal of what we can't and through our speaking/singing, encourages its manifestation. The Bible declares in Proverbs 18:21 that:

"Death and life are in the power of the tongue: and they that love it shall eat the fruit thereof." In other words, if we speak, sing or declare it, we will have what we say! Our words can shape and change our surroundings and atmosphere, so if you speak negativity that's what will always occur. If you speak positive things, look for that to happen. Using our words in the form of songs to sing prophetically is not only Biblical but is encouraged to motivate the Holy Spirit to act on our behalf.

In 2 Chronicles 20th Chapter, King Jehosphat sent the singers (praise team) dressed in their holy priestly garments on the front line before the enemy during war, they would sing *"Praise the Lord, for His mercy endureth forever!"* A very unconventional approach to fighting a war I would add, but God had already assured him that this fight was the Lord's! The Bible declares that God sent ambushments against their enemies by confusing them of who to kill. They believed God would fight their battles for them; and guess what?.....**GOD DID!** They were prophetically releasing songs of praise that God was their refuge and strength; that He was their very present help in time of trouble although they were staring their enemy right in the face. Victory hadn't happened yet, but they knew it would be theirs if they continued to praise God in obedience!

Corporate Worship in that day was focused on encouraging or inviting the presence of the Lord into their environment; they wanted Him to **MANIFEST** Himself as they sang songs, lifted their hands, gave thanks and repented to the Lord. Here are some more scriptures **for you to study** in regards to how Davidic worship was utilized in David's day:

1Chronicles 25:1 and Psalm 46:10; 50:7; 85:8 35:18

(Prophetic Davidic Worship)

Psalm 34:3; 57:5

(Corporate worship within the Tabernacle)

Psalm 33:3; 96:1; 149:1

(Holy Ghost inspired spontaneous songs of worship)

Psalm 30:4; 35:18

(Worship giving thanks unto God)

I Kings 8:11; Chronicles 5:14; Psalm 50:2

(Inviting the manifest presence of God into their worship)

King David was the inventor of MANY instruments (1 Chronicles 23:5). He was a strong influence of development to the worship arts ministry by incorporating singing, prophetic music, the spontaneity of worship, dancing, the playing of tambourines, all at the same time in order to give God utlimate glory.

His (David's) influence of this type of worship became known as **"Davidic Worship"** and continued right on into the reign of Solomon.

I plan to continue deeper into the Davidic worship ministry in another forthcoming book that will be a part of my Worship Arts Book Series, but I think for now, I'll stop here. I do want you to absorb all the content to the degree that you can receive and **UNDERSTAND** what is being said, not to overwhelm you with information.

CHAPTER 7

NOTES

CHAPTER 8

IMPORTANT POINTS TO REMEMBER ABOUT WORSHIP

As you continue to develop your personal relationship with God, I pray that the points brought out in this book will be of valuable help to you. I encourage you to DAILY strengthen your relationship with the Lord by starting your day with prayer with Him, reading the Word for at least 15 -30 minutes a day (maybe on your lunch hour, after you've taken a nap when you get off work, or right before you go to bed at night), but make time for Him everyday He allows you to live. Here are some other very practical but helpful tips to remember about our study on worship:

*Worship is far more than singing or the playing of instruments.

*Always remember your first love (Revelation 2:1-7) and avoid temptations.

*Keep in mind that your DAILY LIFE should be an offering of worship unto God, in the way we behave and speak to others, therefore let worship become your LIFESTYLE!

*True worship should ALWAYS give God glory in some manner; think about this: is God getting any glory out of WHAT you're doing or saying? Hmmm.....

*Worship is **NEVER** about you, but what you can give to God; it's about **RELATIONSHIP with Him.**

*Worship is unselfish in its very essence.

*God **NEVER** shares His glory; He **<u>GETS</u>** the glory!

*Guard your heart with all due diligence in order to keep complacency and stubbornness from settling in. (Jeremiah 13:10).

*Be willing to set aside your personal preferences during corporate worship. Be generous in your giving unto the Lord in your tithes and offerings as well as your giftings and talents. These are all considered sacrificial offerings of modern day worship. We can worship God through our giving (in finances, service & gifts - I Corinthians 16:2; 2 Corinthians 9:6-8), as well as with our time in service to others.

*Always be cheerful, joyful and glad when entering the presence of the Lord; presenting yourself Holy, fully and wholeheartedly.
(Psalm 100:2; 2 Corinthian 9:7).

It is truly my prayer and hope that if you are one that has been struggling with whether you should be a part of your local assembly's worship arts ministry, that this book may have given you some insight on making that decision. Sometimes, understanding the beginnings of a "thing" helps you to understand it even better as to what it has evolved into NOW.

The purpose of me addressing the topics of PRAISE and WORSHIP through this book series separately, is because I wanted to share in the clearest form I could a small history of where these ministries were birthed by doing a brief study on them in the Bible. As I've taught workshops for choirs and praise teams all over the country, I've found that most that serve in those ministries know little to nothing about the basic Biblical background, yet they are steady serving as dancers, singers and praise team members without the wisdom or understanding necessary of how to make their ministry even MORE impactful in service to the Kingdom!

In order for us to be well-rounded servants in our various fields of the worship arts, I think it's important to get a basic understanding of its history, where certain things came from and why it's important to us today. As I continue my writing in the book series, I plan to address the following subjects that may also be of interest to you as a Servant of the Worship Arts Ministry:

*For Worship Leaders & Praise Team Members

*For Musicians

*For Choirs and Choir Members

*For Dance, Banner and Mime Ministers

*A Study on the luciferic Spirit

* Psalm School - A Study on the Book of Psalms

So get ready to CONTINUE studying the Word as it pertains to YOUR area of ministry...the Worship Arts and the impact it has or can have on our local assemblies can be **PHENOMENAL!** Let's try to learn all we can from God's perspective so that we may give Him glory like David did with "all our might" but also through wisdom, in God's order and in accordance to His Word.

My prayer is that God will empower you with His precious Holy Spirit to boldly share and demonstrate your gifts in the area He has called you to. That every platform you are blessed to grace will make way for the manifested presence of the Lord and that He will be glorified through the gifts, talents and Anointing He's laid on your life.

Thank you for reading and caring enough about YOUR CALLING to purchase this book; may it be a blessing and a welcomed reference manual for you as your journey continues in the fabulous Calling of the Worship Arts Ministry.

~**Pastor (Psalmist) Doris Stokes Knight**

CHAPTER 8

NOTES

Be sure to pick up the complementary read to this book, **PRAISE: The Foundation for Servants of the Worship Arts Ministry** to help take you even further into an understanding of the ministry of Praise. Learn what the enemy wants to keep hidden from you to stifle your Anointing and keep you ineffective for God's use in the Kingdom. Also, let me know if either of these books have been a blessing to you! You may email me at: **bpewordpublishing@gmail.com**. I love getting emails from those who appreciate the ministry I offer to the Kingdom be it through my online worship arts workshops, in-person worship arts workshops, concerts and live performances, my Column **"Black Pearls"** or now through the medium of my book series. I'll be sure to respond to your questions or comments.

May God be glorified through **YOU** as you freely RELEASE your Praise unto Him!

Visit my Author's Website to order your copy at:

www.bpewordpublishing.wix.com/Kingdombooks

ABOUT THE AUTHOR:

DORIS STOKES KNIGHT

There are singers and there are SANGERS; Psalmist Doris Stokes just happens to be blessed as one of the latter! This dynamic vocalist and 2010 SIX (6) TIME I HEAR MUSIC Gospel "People's Choice Awards" Winner hails out of the Stokes Family of Dayton, Ohio. She is the youngest member of this star-producing family, possessing a song and style all her own. She has been singing ever since she can remember, starting in church and at home with brothers, Otha (formerly of the group **The Ohio Hustlers** & **The Sugarhill Gang**), Arthur (Hakim, formerly of the Dayton R&B group **"Heatwave"**), Frank, Ralph, Otis (formerly of the R&B group **"Lakeside"**) and sister Diane. The family often sang in huddles in the back room or in the basement of their parents' home. "Otis and Hakim were always in charge of giving out the singing parts to all of us and we would sing some commercial jingle or cartoon theme song in five (5) part harmony."

Doris and her siblings were raised in a Christian home by parents who loved the Lord. "It's really all we knew from the very beginning. My Mom and Dad made us sing in the choir. We were "drafted" into it; once the secret was out that we could all sing! Since going to church was never an option in our household, being in the choir was a requirement that was not open for discussion. Just like school... it was 'understood.'"

Doris began writing songs at the age of nineteen however she first sang professionally on brother Otis' first solo project. During these early years, she also sang background vocals with brother Hakim on several recordings including the soundtrack to the movie, "The Garbage Pail Kids" on MCA/Curb Records.

Soon she began singing Gospel professionally and became a founding member with contemporary gospel choir out of Cincinnati, Ohio "David Minor With One Voice." She went on to lead praise and worship services in penal facilities (prison ministry is her passion) all over the Ohio Valley and the Tri-state areas. "I realize there's nothing glamorous about singing in prison, but you are either Anointed to do it or you're not. I looked beyond the metal bars and barbed wire and realized that Jesus died for them too." Doris was later brought into her oldest brother's music ministry, the late (and dynamic) Gospel saxophonist, Minister Otha Stokes, Jr. until his unexpected passing in June 1999.

Doris' old choir "David Minor With One Voice" which had disbanded in 1997, was re-grouped and re-named "New VisionUnder the Direction of Archie Byers." This group began to make an impressionable impact on the gospel music scene all over Cincinnati, the Tri-state and the southern region. They completed one "live" CD in which Doris was a featured soloist. New Vision opened and/or served as workshop choir for such gospel artists as: **Rodnie Bryant, LaMar Campbell, Marvin Sapp, Dorinda Clark-Cole, Karen Clark-Sheard, Kurt Carr, Tramaine Hawkins, Beverly Crawford** and **Charles Fold** just to name a few.

Doris has fast become a premier guest at workshops, convocations and conferences nationwide! She has also become a TBN "favorite" guest music minister as well as a teacher/clinician on the importance of praise and worship as a lifestyle.

She served as a faithful member of the powerhouse praise and worship background group "Praise" which sang behind former Crystal Rose Records recording artist, **Elder Rodney Posey.**

Doris' other vocal influences include Aretha Franklin, Vanessa Bell Armstrong, Dorinda Clark-Cole, Daryl Coley and Rance Allen. In 2009, Psalmist Doris Stokes was the featured openingArtist for the 2009 Midwest Regional Black Family Reunion at Sawyer Point Park in Cincinnati, OH sponsored by McDonalds. The concert's Special Guest artists were Gospel favorites **Cece Winans & J. Moss.**

The excitement continues to build as she was one of the featured ministries showcased on the 2010 Allstate Gospel Superfest, Executive Produced by **Dr. Bobby Cartwright**. The show was filmed at the Cintas Center on the campus of Xavier University in Cincinnati, Ohio in January 2010 and scheduled for broadcast on the GMC (Gospel Music Channel) on Sunday evenings. She was also featured on the "Back Stage Pass" Television show also produced by Dr. Bobby Cartwright; the show is hosted by Clifton Davis.

Throughout her ministerial career, Doris has shared stages with some of the Gospel industry's finest including **Israel Houghton, Marvin Sapp, the late Dr. Charles Fold, Karen Clark-Sheard, Cece Winans, Mom Winans, Vickie Winans, Elder Carnell Murrel** (of whom is featured on the Reprise of "Calypso Praise")l, **Rance Allen, Father Hayes, J. Moss, Deitrick Haddon, Men of Standard, Fred Hammond, Minister Earl Bynum, Ronnie "Diamond" Hoard, Minister Phillip Carter, Helen Baylor** among many others and has served as background vocalist for such Gospel industry favorites as **Byron Cage** and **Dorinda Clark-Cole.**

In addition to her busy music ministry, Doris is the mother of one son, Nouri whom she adores. She is also a fashion designer (designing most of her stage outfits) and looking to launch a line specifically for women in ministry.

"Without spending a small mint, it can be pretty darn expensive and challenging to find clothing that is ministry appropriate; that is more or less how I got into designing. It's not easy finding affordable, fashionable clothing that is pulpit or stage-ready and appropriate to minister in. You either have to settle for being broke after you've gone shopping or look like Mary Poppins. In my humble opinion, you shouldn't have to settle either way. I think it's VERY possible to be fashionable and appropriately dressed at the same time and STILL have a little change left in your pocket when it's all said and done."

In addition, Doris is a featured Gospel Columnist for the national publications of Gospel Synergy, N'Spiration, Airplay 360, Embrace and Faith Access magazines where she shares her insights and encouragement to make praise and worship a lifestyle with the readers of her column "Black Pearls." She serves as Co-Hosts of two local television programs in the Cincinnati area and is also very active as an actress/vocalist in Gospel stage plays whenever the opportunity arises! She was featured in the gospel play "An Upper Room Experience" which also starred **Shirley Murdock** and has traveled with the God's Champion Entertainment stage production "Someone To Love Me" as the special Guest Psalmist during intermission. Doris is presently writing her own stage production tentatively entitled, "We Are Family…?" She believes this stage version of her testimony will have audiences laughing hysterically one moment and in tears the next. It should also make everyone who sees it inventory themselves on some very key life issues, especially racism in the church.

Doris also teaches a popular ONLINE Worship Arts Workshop for those that serve in the local church in any area of the Worship Arts ministry.

"These courses help to prepare & develop those that have a calling in dance, banner & mime ministries as well as praise & worship teams, worship leaders, choir directors, choir members, musicians and can be taken from the comfort of your OWN HOME. "It's IMPERATIVE that we understand from a Biblical perspective the history of our calling and WHAT it is we're called to do. We can't be effective to the Body if we don't understand what we're doing ourselves" In 2012, she may now add "Author" to her list of credits and responsibilities as she readies herself to release the Praise & Worship Unleashed "Dynamic Duo" series of books based off of her in-person and online Worship Arts Workshops. The books entitled: PRAISE: The Foundation for Servants of the Worship Arts Ministry and WORSHIP: The Foundation for Servants of the Worship Arts Ministry are both designed to help anyone who is seeking to find if their place in service to the Kingdom resides in one of the above areas of the worship arts ministry.

It also educates the reader on the history of where both of these ministries began and helps to enlighten them on why the power behind these two different ministries of service are extremely necessary for placement in our local assemblies as well as incorporated into our daily lives. Both publications should be available by Fall of 2012.

Doris holds a Master's Degree in Christian Education/Church Administration & Organization from International Apostolic University and a Bachelor's Degree in Organizational Management from Wilberforce University .

She is now awaiting conference as a candidate for her Doctorate Degree in Worship Arts & Sacred Music. Her live recording was the culmination and conclusion of her requirements for graduation.

In addition, 2011 has brought forth quite a few notable accomplishments for Psalmist Doris: She debuted her NEW Single "Blow Me Away" on **Bobby Jones Gospel's** 31st Season on the BET Network, she was Guest on **"I'm Just Sayin'** with Pastor Dan Willis which is the #1 Gospel Program on the TCT Network, she taught the praise & worship workshop for Dorinda Clark Cole's Annual Singer's & Musicians' Conference held in Detroit, Michigan, and was elevated in ministry on September 10th (2011) as a Kingdom PASTOR! NO, not as an overseer of a Church body (Senior Pastor), but she does "Pastor" many of those students who have gained education, insight, empowerment, wisdom and inspiration from her Anointed Worship Arts Workshops! She also carries a very quiet but powerful prophetic Anointing on her life. "I'm not one for big talk, titles and licenses. I just believe in walking in order, obedience and humility. If you're real, signs, wonders and the truth will follow; the Word declares that!"

After faithfully supporting and serving others in diverse capacities for so many years, the time has now come for Doris to step out from behind the scenes and move forward in her season of ministry as a TRIPLE THREAT; she's Anointed to preach, teach and sing! Her FIRST "live" solo effort entitled, "Praise & Worship...Unleashed!" was released in January 2009; she is now hard at work on her Sophomore project where the FIRST single "Blow Me Away" was released in October 2011 and received enthusiastically by radio nationwide! The NEW project is being produced by herself and the awesome Michael Mindingall (i.e., Diana Ross, Aretha Franklin, Carnell Murrell, Coko, etc.).

Once you have experienced praise and worship with this Gem, there will be no doubt that you have been in the presence of the Lord and that she IS Anointed! Keep your eyes and ears open for this up and coming princess that hails from the "Gem City." Great things ARE happening for Gospel music's *"Black Pearl"*, **Psalmist Doris Stokes!**

APPENDIX

As a compliment to this book, make sure you order **YOUR COPY** of Psalmist' CD projects: **"Praise & Worship...Unleashed!"**

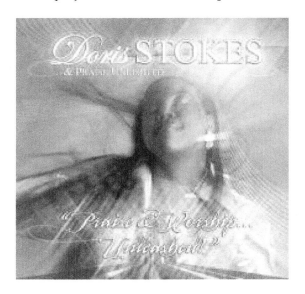

Available ONLINE at:

Available ONLINE at:
www.itunes.apple.com/us/artist/psalmist-doris-stokes
www.cdbaby.com/cd/dorisastokes2
and <u>ALL</u> major ONLINE music outlets!

The CURRENT Single "Blow Me Away!"

Available ONLINE at:
www.itunes.apple.com/us/artist/psalmist-doris-stokes
www.cdbaby.com/cd/dorisastokes2
and ALL major ONLINE music outlets!

Doris Stokes Knight, also lovingly known as Psalmist Doris Stokes, is available for the following Anointed ministry services:

*Ordained Kingdom Pastor
*Anointed Speaker/Preacher of the Gospel
*Guest Psalmist for Convocations, Conferences, Anniversaries, etc.
*Worship Leader
*Stage Hostess (MC) for Concerts and Programs
*Songwriting/Music Production
*Worship Arts Workshop Clinician (In Person and ONLINE Courses)
*Praise & Worship Team Development
*Vocal Coaching
*Background Vocalist

To Book (Psalmist) Doris Stokes Knight for YOUR next event, or for an IN-PERSON Worship Arts Workshop, please contact:
Mr. Bruce Knight
Management for (Psalmist) Doris Stokes Knight
P.O. Box 18061
Fairfield, OH 45018
Email: **bpewordpublishing@gmail.com**
Official Website: **www.bpewordpublishing.wix.com/Kingdombooks**

Answers To The Pre -"WORSHIP" Quiz

True or False?

1.   An **effective worship leader** always makes sure each of the praise team members' outfits are nice and color-coordinated.   False
Chapter 1 – What Praise & Worship IS NOT!

2.   Consecration is not a requirement that needs to be met in order to worship God.   False
Chapter 2 – Worship 101 – What Is Worship?

3.   The desire for true worship begins inside of our own selves.   True
Chapter 2 – Worship 101 – What Is Worship?

4.   In the Old Testament, Aaron was in charge of the construction of the Tabernacle.   False
Chapter 3 - Who Has The Ability to Worship?

5.   **Moses** was the designer of the Old Testament Tabernacle.   True
Chapter 3 – Who Has The Ability to Worship?

6.   The **"Holy of Holies"** is where the High Priest lived.   False
Chapter 3 – Who Has The Ability to Worship?

7.   The Ark of the Covenant was welcomed by all who saw it   False
Chapter 3 – Who Has The Ability to Worship?

8.   Obed-edom was afraid of the Ark of the Covenant, therefore it was taken to King David's house to reside for three months.   False
Chapter 3 – Who Has The Ability to Worship?

9.   The Ark of the Covenant is where Noah lived.   False
Chapter 3 – Who Has The Ability to Worship?

10.   Worshipers are **Anointed** by their pastors.   False
Chapter 4 – WORSHIP A Deeper Understanding

22March2013
ISBN - 13: 978-1466487567
ISBN - 10: 1466487569

Printed in Great Britain
by Amazon